Robert Lawson

Twayne's United States Authors Series

Ruth K. MacDonald, Editor

TUSAS 686

ROBERT LAWSON, 1941.
Photograph by Hansel Meith.

Robert Lawson

Gary D. Schmidt

Calvin College

Twayne Publishers
An Imprint of Simon & Schuster Macmillan
New York

Prentice Hall International
London • Mexico City • New Delhi • Singapore • Sydney • Toronto

Twayne's United States Authors Series No. 686

Robert Lawson
Gary D. Schmidt

Copyright © 1997 by Twayne Publishers

Twayne Publishers
An Imprint of Simon & Schuster Macmillan
1633 Broadway
New York, NY 10019

AU **Library of Congress Cataloging-in-Publication Data**

Schmidt, Gary D.
        Robert Lawson / Gary D. Schmidt.
            p. cm. — (Twayne's United States authors series ; TUSAS 686)
        Includes bibliographical references and index.
        ISBN 0-8057-4585-8 (alk. paper)
        1. Lawson, Robert, 1892–1957—Criticism and interpretation.
    2. Children's stories, American—History and criticism.
    3. Children's stories, American—Illustrations.   I. Title.
    II. Series.
    PS3523.A9548Z88   1997
    813'.52—dc21   97-21000
                                                                                                            CIP

10 9 8 7 6 5 4 3 2 1

Printed in the United States of America

For Otto Marx
In memory of a life of prayer and love

Contents

Preface

Any book that deals with the life and work of Robert Lawson must in some measure justify itself. Aside from *Rabbit Hill* and *The Tough Winter,* which he both illustrated and wrote, and *The Story of Ferdinand* and *Mr. Popper's Penguins,* which he illustrated, Lawson's work has passed into some oblivion, despite his status as the only winner of both the Newbery and Caldecott awards. Few would recognize titles such as *The Roving Lobster* or *The Wee Men of Ballywooden,* which he illustrated back in the 1930s, or even his more recent work: *Smeller Martin, Mr. Wilmer, Mr. Twigg's Mistake,* or *The Great Wheel.* Yet in his own time, now almost half a century ago, he was much admired. He rarely received even a mediocre review.

Certainly there are some difficulties in Lawson's work. Much of it is dated in a peculiarly difficult way: references to World War II, to the rationing of the period, and even to fashions of the period make the books remote and at times inaccessible to a child audience. Some of the books are simply ill-conceived, written by a man who was a commercial artist paid by the piece. And not a little of Lawson's drawing is less than one might expect by a major illustrator. In 1946, after 15 years of drawing primarily fantasy work, he wrote that he did not particularly care to draw "ordinary modern people," a cryptic whine that perhaps hides the fact that his figures are not distinguished. Sometimes, wrote his editor at Little, Brown, his people "seem little more than patterns."[1] Often they seem to be staged, posturing awkwardly for a painter to capture them. He does, however, have what his editor called an "ease with animal symmetry," and no one who has read *The Story of Ferdinand* (by Munro Leaf) could argue with the successful lines of Lawson's animal forms (Jones, 22).

A more disagreeable problem is Lawson's handling of his African-American characters. Certainly his depictions are of a piece with the kind of portrayals that were typical of the 1940s and 1950s, but today they strike a harsh and discordant note. In *They Were Strong and Good*, Lawson has the unenviable task of trying to explain why his father never considered the young boy who was his slave as, particularly, a slave; he seems merely a hunting companion who is part of the household. But the wording of his text suggests a disturbing sense of ownership: "When my father was very young he had two dogs and a colored boy. The dogs were named Sextus Hostilius and Numa Pompilius. The colored boy was just my father's age. He was a slave, but they didn't call him that. They just called him Dick."[2] This text has been revised since then, but it is truly a text that cannot be recovered. The revision seeks to eliminate the semantic sleight of hand about slavery, but it nevertheless retains the sense of ownership:"When my father was very young he had a Negro slave and two dogs. The dogs were named Sextus Hostilius and Numa Pompilius. The Negro boy was just my father's age and his name was Dick." The ready acceptance of slavery, the refusal to question, is most problematic, especially in a book focusing on the strong and good people that grew a country. One can hardly imagine such a text being written today, and perhaps this explains why this Caldecott-winning work is so rarely on the shelves of bookstores.

And yet elements of Lawson's work make him an important figure to study. His work sprawls across 30 years of this century. He illustrated almost 50 works by other writers and 20 works of his own. He, together with artists like Robert McCloskey and James Daugherty, defined the styles of children's literature for the middle part of the century. And like those artists, Lawson had a vision to impart; he wanted to tell about the American spirit, not in a historical sense but in an impressionistic sense. He would tell about it through his nonsense, through his historical fantasies, through his "pageants." Lawson was a writer and illustrator with a sense that he had a role to fill in children's literature: he was to tell about America at a time when America was experiencing real difficulties—in the middle of a troubled century, during the advent of a world war.

What makes Lawson particularly worthy of study 40 years after his last book is his experimentation with genres and their boundaries. Lawson's innovations, his blurring of generic distinctions, led to new and surprising kinds of narratives. He invented genres, ruptured their boundaries, and suited them to his own purposes. In telling the stories of figures like Christopher Columbus and Benjamin Franklin, he invented historical fantasy to twist the stories into new directions. When he wanted to tell a realistic story of a boy and his pet, he added fantasy to give the tale an entirely new level, playing with the realistic and fantasy elements so that they intertwined and mingled. When he wanted to write about the rabbits that he saw all around him in Connecticut, he merged fantasy with realism yet again to talk about a vision of the natural world. The examination of this experimentation is the focus of this study.

After the biographical sketch presented in Chapter 1, my analysis is for the most part by genre. In Chapter 2, however, I focus on two works that seem to epitomize Lawson's feelings about America: the autobiographical *They Were Strong and Good* and his historical "pageant," *Watchwords of Liberty*. Chapter 3 examines Lawson's "biographies" of figures as told by their pets; it focuses on how the shift to the fantasy perspective affects the traditional understanding of the figure's life story. Chapter 4, about the Rabbit Hill books, looks at the combination of autobiography, realism, and fantasy, and how this combination leads to an impassioned plea for tolerance. Chapter 5 discusses Lawson's merging of formulas usually reserved for the genre of realism with fantasy elements. (Owing to space limitations, I do not discuss Lawson's autobiographical *At That Time* and *Country Colic,* works whose target audiences are arguably not children.)

Lawson saw no distinction between his work as writer and illustrator; from his earliest article he showed an awareness that the two must work together to create a total effect. For this reason this study also focuses especially on the interaction of text and illustration in Lawson's work, examining the ways in which that interaction became a vehicle for Lawson's message about American life. Chapter 6 looks at this interaction in his collaborative works, while Chapter 7 examines the union of message with form in his final book.

This study takes seriously Lawson's claims about his audience: "I have never changed one conception or line or detail to suit the supposed age of the reader. And I have never, in what writing I have done, changed one word or phrase of text because I felt it might be over the heads of children. I have never, I hope, insulted the intelligence of any child."[3] Now there may have been times when Lawson might have profited by a change in conception or line. But his concern for audience, his refusal to "write down," was something that marked his work, sometimes problematically but sometimes brilliantly. This question of audience relates directly to his handling of genre and thus figures in each chapter.

A study of works, many of which are out of print and inaccessible, naturally draws upon the skills of those librarians at Calvin College who, yet again, have shown their generosity of spirit and willingness to accommodate even the most unreasonable plea. For that I thank Conrad Bult, the Assistant Director of Calvin College's Hekman Library, and Kathleen Struck, the patient wonder of the Interlibrary Loan office, for all their assistance.

The greatest thanks of all go, again, to Anne, who watched this book develop during a time of no little upheaval.

Chronology

1892   Robert Lawson is born 4 October in New York City to William Bethel and Elma Cecilia (Bowman) Lawson.

1911   Enters New York School of Fine and Applied Arts, later known as the Parsons School of Design.

1915   Begins freelance illustration work with *Harper's Weekly, The Delineator,* and *Vogue.*

1917   Travels to France to serve in the Camouflage section of the 40th Engineers of the American Expeditionary Force.

1919   Resumes his career in commercial illustration, adding *The Designer, Century,* and *Pictorial Review.*

1922   Marries Marie Abrams 6 September; illustrates George Randolph Chester's *The Wonderful Adventures of Little Prince Toofat.*

1923   Moves to Westport, Connecticut; begins to illustrate greeting cards.

1930   Begins career in etching; illustrates Arthur Mason's *The Wee Men of Ballywooden.*

1931   Wins the John Taylor Arms prize of the Society of American Etchers. Illustrates Arthur Mason's "Moving of the Bog," Margery Williams Bianco's "The House That Grew Small," and Louis Untermeyer's "The Donkey of God" for *Saint Nicholas Magazine*; Arthur Mason's *From the Horn of the Moon* and *The Roving Lobster.*

1932   Illustrates Ella Young's *The Unicorn with Silver Shoes* and Barbara Ring's *Peik.*

1933   Returns to live in New York City. Illustrates Margery Williams Bianco's *The Hurdy-Gurdy Man* and John Marquand's *Haven's End.*

1934   Illustrates William Wister Haines's *Slim* and W. W. Tarn's *Treasure of the Isle of Mist.*

1935   Illustrates Elizabeth Coatsworth's *The Golden Horseshoe* and Emma Gelders Sterne's *Drums of Monmouth*.

1936   Returns to Westport, Connecticut, and builds "Rabbit Hill." Illustrates Helen Dixon Bates's *Betsy Ross* and *Francis Scott Key*, Elizabeth Gales's *Seven Beads of Wampum*, Munro Leaf's *The Story of Ferdinand*, and Mabelle Glenn's *Tunes and Harmonies*.

1937   Illustrates Ruth Barnes's *I Hear America Singing: An Anthology of Folk Poetry*, Walter Russell Bowie's *The Story of Jesus for Young People*, Clarence Stratton's *Swords and Statues*, Mark Twain's *The Prince and the Pauper*, Maribelle Cormack's *Wind of the Vikings*, John E. Brewton's *Under the Tent of the Sky*, Jean Rosmer's *In Secret Service*, Emma Gelders Sterne's *Miranda Is a Princess*, Helen Dean Fish's *Four and Twenty Blackbirds*, and Rita Kissin's *Pete the Pelican*.

1938   Wins Caldecott Honor for illustrating Helen Dean Fish's *Four and Twenty Blackbirds*. Illustrates Richard and Florence Atwater's Newbery-winning *Mr. Popper's Penguins*, Eleanor Farjeon's *One Foot in Fairyland*, Munro Leaf's *Wee Gillis*, William Wister Haines's *High Tension*, and Charles Dickens's *A Tale of Two Cities*. *The Story of Ferdinand* is adapted for film by Walt Disney.

1939   Wins Caldecott Honor for illustrating Munro Leaf's *Wee Gillis*. *Ben and Me*. Illustrates John Bunyan's *Pilgrim's Progress* and the endpages for T. H. White's *The Sword in the Stone*.

1940   *Just for Fun: A Collection of Stories and Verses* and *They Were Strong and Good*. Illustrates John E. Brewton's *Gaily We Parade*.

1941   Wins Caldecott Medal for *They Were Strong and Good*. *I Discover Columbus*. Illustrates Munro Leaf's *The Story of Simpson and Sampson* and *Aesop's Fables*.

1942   Illustrates Elizabeth Janet Gray's Newbery-winning *Adam of the Road*, C. S. Forester's *Poo-Poo and the Dragons*, Andrew Lang's *Prince Prigio*, and James Stephens's *The Crock of Gold*.

1943   *Watchwords of Liberty.* Illustrates Val Teal's *The Little Woman Wanted Noise.*

1944   *Country Colic* and *Rabbit Hill.*

1945   Wins Newbery Award for *Rabbit Hill. Mr. Wilmer.* Illustrates William Hall's *The Shoelace Robin.*

1946   Illustrates Tom Robinson's *Greylock and the Robins.*

1947   *At That Time* and *Mr. Twigg's Mistake.*

1948   *Robbut: A Tale of Tails.*

1949   *Dick Whittington and His Cat* and *The Fabulous Flight.*

1950   *Smeller Martin.* Illustrates Francis F. Winthrop's *Benjamin Franklin.*

1951   *McWhinney's Jaunt.*

1952   *Edward, Hoppy and Joe.* Illustrates Mary Potter's *Mathematics for Success.*

1953   *Mr. Revere and I.*

1954   *The Tough Winter. Ben and Me* is adapted for film by Walt Disney.

1956   Marie Lawson dies. *Captain Kidd's Cat.*

1957   Robert Lawson dies 26 May. *The Great Wheel.*

1958   Wins Newbery Honor for *The Great Wheel.*

1961   Wins Lewis Carroll Shelf Award for *Ben and Me.*

1963   Wins Lewis Carroll Shelf Award for *Rabbit Hill.*

1967   *Rabbit Hill* adapted for film by NBC.

Chapter One
Master of Rabbit Hill

On 9 June 1945, in the midst of one of the most tumultuous weeks of the century, Robert Lawson stood up in a Waldorf-Astoria banquet room to receive the Newbery Medal for *Rabbit Hill*. He was familiar with the awards luncheon given by the American Library Association, as he had been there four years earlier to receive the Caldecott Medal for *They Were Strong and Good*. His acceptance speech was humble and humorous. The award, he insisted, should be divided into pieces to be shared with his wife; his editor, May Massee; and the production designer, Morris Colman. And the largest piece should go to Little Georgie, the protagonist, "who wrote the thing, because I don't remember doing that at all."[1]

One of the opening paragraphs of the speech says much about Lawson's approach to his writing: "This seems to have been quite a season for rabbits, what with Harvey receiving the Pulitzer Prize and Little Georgie the Newbery. It has been a good spring for them in the arts, but a pretty miserable one for them out of doors. What with the cold weather and all the rain they look pretty bedraggled. They all seemed to have a worried air, too, as well they might, for after all, they're one of the few things that are still ration point free" ("Newbery," 233–34). The humor of the last line is directed at an adult audience at a particular point in time—about a war hardship they were all enduring—but more important is the easy and almost imperceptible movement back and forth between reality and fantasy. The rabbits depicted in the arts—Little Georgie and Harvey—are no less real than the rabbits that are having a damp spring. And those wild rabbits also live between reality and fantasy; they all, Lawson suggests, have a worried air.

Lawson's willingness to merge realism with fantasy was absolutely central to his work in children's literature, and was a large part of the experimentation he conducted on the boundaries of the genres within which he worked. His realistic stories about a young boy who misses his parents (*Smeller Martin* [1950]), a young boy with an unusual pet (*Mr. Twigg's Mistake* [1945]), or an adult who is trapped in an apparently meaningless life (*Mr. Wilmer* [1945]) are merged with fantastical ele-

1

ments: Davey Martin can identify almost anything by its smell, Squirt Appleton has a gargantuan mole for a pet, and Mr. Wilmer can speak with animals. Lawson's historical tales are similarly built around fantastic motifs; each is narrated by an animal connected with Christopher Columbus, Benjamin Franklin, Captain Kidd, or Paul Revere. Even the Rabbit Hill books merge genres; on the one hand they are animal stories with the fantasy element of talking animals. On the other hand they are realistic tales of life on a country estate. Lawson's most important literary work comes in his experimentation with genres, his willingness to merge conventions to form something quite new—like historical fantasy—and to use it to explore characters and perspectives.

Along with this experimentation, however, came a consistent and dominant theme: America. Many of the early works that he illustrated for others focus on the life of young America; this illustrative motif was important in his writing as well. His historical fantasies all center on the history of America, all pointing to the greatness not only of the American experiment, but of the land itself. Freedom, liberty, the courage to fight for independence—these are the virtues celebrated in Robert Lawson's books. They appear as well in the whimsical fantasies, where Professor McWhinney travels across the face of America, past its national grandeur. The American experiment would also be the theme of some of his earliest original work, such as *They Were Strong and Good* (1941), and it would continue through *Watchwords of Liberty*, which he revised in 1957, the year of his sudden death.

Lawson's life was not marked by the early sense of purpose that one might expect of the only writer and illustrator to receive both the Newbery and Caldecott awards. He was 47 when his first book as writer and illustrator was published: *Ben and Me* (1939). He had, until that time, been both a commercial artist and an illustrator of children's books by other writers, although even that latter interest did not begin until he was 30 years old. "I did not, as a child," he wrote, "have any particular interest in drawing and did none until my last year in High School, when it was pointed out to me that I must prepare to do something in the world. I have always had a vague idea that I would like to be an engineer and build bridges, but since I had managed to avoid every form of mathematics this career did not seem very possible."[2] His interest in engineering was inspired by his reading of Richard Harding Davis's stories, but this "something" to inspire him came in 1908, and it was not by fortuitous circumstances, an encouraging parent, or a mentor. He was inspired by a high school poster contest, which he entered and won with the first drawing he had ever produced. The one-dollar prize represented his first earnings.

This author and illustrator who would write and draw the landscape of America lived, all his life, within a very small area. He was born 4 October 1892 in New York City. He remained there only a short time before his family moved over the Hudson River to Montclair, New Jersey, where Lawson was to spend his childhood. Even though he himself would not envision illustration as significant to his own life, his parents certainly brought him to encounters with story and art. As he recalled: "My mother taught me to like good books. She never forbade my reading trashy books or the funny papers, she didn't care what I read, as long as I was reading something. But she always gave me the finest books that could be had, with the most beautiful illustrations. She always spoke of trashy reading as 'sculch.' The books she read herself, both English and French, were always good books and she talked about them so interestingly and so lovingly that I just naturally got to like good books better than 'sculch.' " Lawson's father was not so much a reader as a storyteller. Coming from Alabama, he enjoyed the dialect of the Uncle Remus stories, and he read them to his son often. He also told Lawson stories of the Civil War, in which he had fought at the age of 15.[3]

Lawson's early exposure to story was accompanied by an exposure to art. The family's Montclair house was where the American landscape painter George Innes spent his last 20 years. With his brother, Lawson shared the room that had been Innes's studio—a room he described as "very pleasant": "I thought it would be nice to be an artist and work in a big, airy room like that" (quoted in Weston, 75). Lawson's father disagreed; he hoped that Lawson would go into the drygoods business. But his mother was an artist herself, and once a year she took young Lawson to New York City, where they would spend the day in the Metropolitan Museum of Fine Art. When he was only three or four, she took him to France; years later, Lawson would recall a rainy-day visit to Napoleon's tomb. As she had with his reading, Lawson's mother allowed him to judge for himself: "She never told me what I should like or shouldn't like, we just looked at everything and had a grand time" (quoted in Weston, 75).

In 1911, Lawson came to the point where he had to decide whether he should indeed follow his father and find a safe, prosperous profession, or whether he should follow the artistic tendencies that his mother had nurtured so liberally. Rejecting college, he decided to enter art school, although the decision was a tentative one; his wife would later suggest that art school for Lawson was "more of a trial than the definite adoption of a profession."[4] He entered the New York School of Fine and Applied Arts, later called the Parsons School of Design, and after securing scholarships in life drawing and—more importantly for his later career—illustration, he studied for two years under Ray Sloan Bredin and Howard Giles.

When he finished, he began looking about for commissions, securing his first one with *Harper's Weekly*. His first published drawing appeared in the 30 January 1915 issue of that journal, a full-page illustration of a poem on the invasion of Belgium. He also illustrated a series of "Framers of the Constitution of the USA" ads for Budweiser, perhaps foreshadowing his later interest in historical subjects. Lawson's first published text appears in a December 1915 issue of *Harper's Weekly,* in which he describes a "powder town" being constructed in New Jersey. He accompanies it with a rough sketch of the town. For the next three years Lawson illustrated for *Harper's Weekly,* as well as *The Delineator* and *Vogue.*

At the same time he took on an assortment of jobs as he tried to establish himself as an artist: "[I] designed scenery and costumes for the Washington Square Players, costumed and directed a large pageant, did book plates, tried some portraits. I even designed a house for a woman, who through some error thought I was an architect. And what's more, she liked it."[5] With the Washington Square Players, later known as the Theatrical Guild, Lawson worked with Robert E. Jones, known for his dramatic color and lighting in imaginative sets that graced productions of Eugene O'Neill plays, as well as Lee Simonson and Joseph B. Platt. Under their influence, Lawson began to consider a career in landscape painting. He was 25, and had not yet found a direction.

But in 1917, Lawson left Greenwich Village, where he had worked since art school, and traveled to France, where he served in the Camouflage section of the 40th Engineers. He was there for a year and a half, before returning to take up his interrupted career as a commercial artist. In his own words, he took up his career again "earnestly" ("Robert Lawson," 285). *Harper's Weekly* had succumbed in 1916, but Lawson began to draw for *The Delineator* again, and he added *The Designer, Century,* and *Pictorial Review.* On one level this turn was yet another delay in his career: it led to extensive work in advertising. Years later, Marie Lawson remembered the drive toward this aspect of his career: "His first fine drawings were for the old *Designer* magazine—full pages in color, filled with delicate detail, humor, and a rich imagination. Everything about them pointed to book illustration, but the Great Boom had come, and these drawings caught the eye of the advertising magnates" (M. Lawson, 240).

Lawson devoted all of his energies to commercial drawing, although he took time to craft six Arthur Rackham–like plates for George Randolph Chester's *The Wonderful Adventures of Little Prince Toofat,* a story that had been serialized in *The Delineator* from June 1917 to March 1922. He filled the margins with very light illustrations of the fanciful wee men that would mark his early work, and with a towering castle motif that resembles the opening to *The Story of Ferdinand.* But this was an anomaly; Lawson was not at this time working consistently in book illustration, but in advertising. And yet, it was not lost time. Those years, Marie wrote, "have never been regretted, for the very limitations and requirements imposed brought a greater technical versatility, more accurate observance of detail, a finer draughtmanship" (M. Lawson, 240). It was, nonetheless, a very long apprenticeship.

If the onset of the Great Depression can be said to have had any good effects, certainly one of them would be the forced change in Robert Lawson's career. He had married Marie Abrams in 1922; she, too, was an artist and illustrator, and as Lawson continued his commercial work, together they began to produce greeting cards. In 1923 they moved up to Westport, Connecticut, and together they drew cards at the rate of one a day for three years until their new home was paid for. But with the Depression the commercial work fell off, and there followed a series of very lean years for the Lawsons. As 1930 approached, Lawson's thirty-eighth year, he found himself forced to change his vision of his art. Marie recalled this time in a positive sense: "The advertising world was a burst balloon. For the first time there was leisure enough to try etching, a medium which, because of its technical challenge, had long attracted him" (M. Lawson, 240). But Lawson remembered this as a time of scrambling: "All this work ceased with the Depression, so I took up etching and worked very hard at it for two or three years, gaining some recognition in that field, but very little money" ("Robert Lawson," 285). In fact, Lawson produced 31 etchings, had two one-man shows in New York City, and in 1931 won the John Taylor Arms prize of the Society of American Etchers, Arms suggesting that "Lawson has explored an entirely new field of subject matter and one untouched by any other etcher in the country—the field of gnomes and fairies, of elves and goblins and sprites, of the cluricaune, the leprechaun and the merrow" (Jones, 110). The next year the society asked him to produce the annual member plate, and he etched a flying horse attended by wee folks who are putting shoes on him; the caption reads "We fix flats."[6] But the John Taylor Arms prize did not establish an income.

By 1933 the Lawsons had little money and felt that they had lost their connections in New York. They sold the house in Westport and returned to the city, where Lawson spent three years trying to renew those connections. To tide them over, Lawson left etching and returned to commercial art; he drew for the *Herald Tribune Magazine* and illustrated textbooks for Ginn and Company in Boston. His work for the *Herald Tribune* was particularly fortunate. May Massee, who would later move to Viking and be Lawson's editor there, was in 1939 an editor at Doubleday, Doran. She was working with Arthur Mason on *The Wee Men of Ballywooden* and having difficulty in finding an illustrator who could match Mason's conception of the illustrations. She had thought of Lawson, whom she had known in the early 1920s, but she had lost contact with him, understandably since he was not working in her field. She had also come to believe that he had died. Lawson recalled their next meeting in his Caldecott acceptance speech for *They Were Strong and Good*: "The Wee Men immediately got to work and arranged things so that very Sunday she happened to see a drawing of mine in the *Herald Tribune Magazine*. She promptly called me on the telephone and found that I was not at all dead. In fact, I was a little hurt by the inquiry."[7]

Massee's decision seems to have been influenced both by the *Herald Tribune Magazine* illustration and some illustrations that Lawson drew to accompany Carl Sandberg's "Rootabaga Stories" that had appeared in *The Designer*. But in these years Massee was also eager to become more cosmopolitan, to expand the boundaries of artists that had traditionally been called upon to illustrate children's books. This was the period when Massee was bringing in European artists like Edgar Parin and Ingri D'Aulaire from Norway and Maud and Miska Petersham from Hungary. She was also bringing in artists who had never before illustrated a children's book, artists like C. B. Falls, James Daugherty, Elizabeth Mac-Kinstry, and now Robert Lawson. She offered him the opportunity to illustrate *The Wee Men of Ballywooden*. "Nothing could have been more fortuitous," wrote Marie. "The turning point had come" (M. Lawson, 241). Lawson's memory of that beginning was more subdued: "I also did a few children's books and gradually they began to occupy most of my time" ("Robert Lawson," 287). It was indeed a turning point, and children's books did indeed begin to occupy most of his time. In 1930, at the age of 38, Lawson had found his career. As she was to do a decade later with Robert McCloskey, May Massee had pointed the way.

Over the next three decades, Lawson was taken up with illustrating children's literature. *The Wee Men of Ballywooden* came out in 1930; in 1931 he illustrated two more Mason books: *From the Horn of the Moon* and *The Roving Lobster.* He also turned to *Saint Nicholas Magazine,* where in July of 1931 an excerpt from Mason's *From the Horn of the Moon* was published, together with four of Lawson's illustrations for that story. In the September issue of *Saint Nicholas* he illustrated Margery Williams Bianco's "The House That Grew Small," about an abandoned house that makes its way down a hill, growing smaller all the while until it is only a dollhouse and adopted by some children; the illustrations combine landscape with whimsy. Finally, in December, he illustrated Louis Untermeyer's "The Donkey of God," a folkloric tale of Saint Francis. Each of the stories was adorned with four or five illustrations, suited to Lawson's emerging skills as a fantasist.

In 1932 Lawson began to expand the number of publishers for whom he worked. The Mason books attracted the attention of Bertha Gunterman, who was beginning to specialize in children's books for Longmans, Green. She offered Lawson the contract for the American edition of Ella Young's *The Unicorn with Silver Shoes.* Also in 1932, Lawson illustrated Barbara Ring's *Peik* for Little, Brown; although he was never attached to a single publishing company, he would continue to work with Little, Brown for the rest of his career. The illustrations for *Peik* led to a commission to illustrate John P. Marquand's *Haven's End* the next year. In 1933 he illustrated two more books, including Margery William Bianco's *The Hurdy-Gurdy Man* for Oxford University Press, and in 1934 and 1935 he illustrated four books for four different presses, three of which were new to his work. In 1936, his reputation as an illustrator growing, Lawson produced four new books with three new publishers, including *The Story of Ferdinand* with Viking Press; together Viking and Little, Brown would account for most of Lawson's important illustration. And in 1937 Lawson produced an astonishing nine titles with seven different publishers, four of which were new to him. It was a remarkably productive era; children's books had indeed come to take up much of his time.

This was also a period in which Lawson was thinking about the crafting of story as well, although he had not yet written a children's story text. In a speech before the Scottish Branch of English Association, Lawson focused on the novel and fairy tale. He spoke of folk tales as the stories of childhood not to diminish them, but to speak of their powerful influence: "The true hero in all the folk tales and fairy tales is not the younger son, or the younger daughter, or the stolen princess, or the ugly duckling, but the soul of man. It was a world where a great deal of discomfort and sorrow had to be borne, and where the most useful virtue was . . . daring, boldness, originality, brains—because people who made [folk tales] realized that the hope of humanity lay not in passivity but in action." He went on to identify the virtues of the Victorian novels that, he argued, sprang from an awareness of folklore. First, those novels tell a good story with gripping drama; second, they develop characters as true types and make judgments about those characters; third, they reproduce reality not through "an inventory of details but [through] a judicious selection"; fourth, their narrators are more interested in the events than in their own reactions to those events; and fifth, each of the great Victorian novels has a purpose, a creed to suggest.[8]

Lawson's optimistic vision of folklore would find its way into his own work; each of his characters is certainly original, and many are bold and daring. But his comments about Victorian novels would also play a role in his later writings. They, too, are stories that are designed to grip the reader quickly, and they are full of "characters," although Lawson is gentle in his judgments of them. His comments on the narrators of Victorian novels are incorrect in terms of those novels—few today would argue that these narrators keep their responses distant from the reader—but those comments are good descriptions of Lawson's narrators, who do maintain a distance, except in the first-person novels.

Most important in terms of his career as an illustrator, however, is Lawson's sense that the novels reproduced reality through a judicious selection of details: this could describe Lawson's mode of illustration. There will be the occasional detailed landscape, an impulse that remained from his Greenwich Village days, but most of the illustrations would be marked by a selection of details rather than a fully reproduced setting.

In 1936 the Lawsons returned to Westport, Connecticut. There they built their home on Weston Road and dubbed it "Rabbit Hill." James Daugherty lived just a few fields away from the Lawsons, and Armstrong Sperry just a few miles away. The Lawsons were to live and work in this house for the rest of their lives, and with books like *Rabbit Hill* and *The Tough Winter,* the real house and Lawson's fictional conception of it were merged.

By the return to Westport, Lawson had illustrated 15 books over six years; outside of *The Hurdy-Gurdy Man* and John P. Marquand's *Haven's End,* few of these are remembered. But 1936 was to bring Lawson together with Munro Leaf—again under the guidance of May Massee—and together they were to produce the book that would truly establish Lawson's career as an illustrator: *The Story of Ferdinand.* Leaf, an editor and director of F. A. Stokes, and his wife, Margaret, had become friends with the Lawsons during the early 1930s. Marie had designed several book jackets for Stokes, and Leaf had promised Lawson that he would write a book for him to illustrate. One Sunday afternoon in October 1935, he wrote all 800 words of the story in just 40 minutes. He chose a bull because he wanted to write about an uncommon animal; he chose the name Ferdinand because King Ferdinand was the only Spanish figure he knew. They brought the book to the Lawsons. Margaret Leaf later recalled that Lawson was so enthusiastic that he began the dummy that evening.[9] But this was not Lawson's recollection: "I laughed over it and told him how swell I thought it was—for someone else" (quoted in Jones, 22). But Leaf persisted.

Lawson was flummoxed by the challenge of it. He had expected a book that would be peopled with the characters of fantasy that he had so frequently drawn. But here was something quite different: "I had never drawn a bull in my life and the problems of drawing a bull with expressions and emotions at various ages seemed impossible" (quoted in Weston, 77). The problem clearly occupied Lawson's mind for some time, and in fact it affected his whole conception of illustration. Two months later, in an article for *Publishers Weekly,* he wrote that an illustrator should "steep himself in the atmosphere of the book and then transfer that feeling in his drawings."[10] The difficulty for Lawson was that he, like Leaf, had never been to Spain and was hardpressed to "steep himself in the atmosphere of the book." But he knew he must. He recalled that "after a couple of months, though, I really had to do something about it. I went to the library and got every picture and book that I could find about Spain and bulls and bullfighting. I studied Spanish landscape, Spanish architecture, bull anatomy, the costumes of Picadores, Matadores, Banderillos, their horses, trappings, and private lives" (quoted in Jones, 22). And so the book took on shape, as his feelings were transferred, with the aid of library study.

The book did not have an auspicious beginning. The dummy, today held in the Frederick R. Gardner Collection of the Free Library of Philadelphia, carries an imprint of So and So press, and the ambiguity of that name seems to have foretold the difficulties of placing the book. Leaf and Lawson first offered the book to Little, Brown, but it was turned down there. They then went to May Massee at Viking, who had to use all her persuasive powers (which were considerable) at Viking to have even a small print run of 5,200 copies accepted.[11]

The publisher was only mildly enthusiastic about the book. Civil War erupted in Spain, and Harold Ginsberg, president of Viking, suggested holding back publication until "the world settles down" (quoted in Leaf, 33). But Massee persisted, despite the fact that all of the advertising money for that session had been allocated to William Pène du Bois's *Giant Otto,* the book that Viking was most enthusiastic about. "*Ferdinand* is a nice little book," suggested Ginsberg, "but *Giant Otto* will live forever."[12] Early reviews were not inspiring, and the book slipped past the Christmas season without making much of a mark. It appeared that Ginsberg's prediction would be right. But soon after Christmas, the book seemed to be discovered. Sales jumped to one hundred copies a week, then two hundred, until by 1937 eight editions had been published; by 1938 the book was selling at a rate of three thousand copies a week. In December of that year it replaced *Gone with the Wind* at the top of the best-seller lists. Margaret Leaf later recalled her bafflement: "It was a complete mystery to us how in the world it happened" (Leaf, 33).

For the Lawsons, *The Story of Ferdinand* was a boon, representing financial security. Within a very short time Ferdinand appeared as a balloon in the Macy's Thanksgiving Day Parade, appeared in a song that made the hit parade, and found the backing of Eleanor Roosevelt, who, while speaking at the Newbery Award dinner to honor Ruth Sawyer's *Roller Skates,* admitted that she hadn't read the book to be honored, but she had recently read *The Story of Ferdinand*; the president had ordered a copy for the White House. The book was soon translated into 60 languages; Walt Disney produced an Oscar-winning eight-and-a-half-minute film of the book, and it was marketed into toys, jewelry, dress material, and games. A spread in the 28 November 1938 *Life* includes photographs of Ferdinand as a bric-a-brac bull, an image on a cereal box and milk glass, a sidewalk toy, a decoration on a lady's hat, and a picture on the side of a balloon. Leaf and Lawson, the short accompanying article suggests, "stand to profit heavily by licensing the use of Ferdinand's image on articles for sale."[13]

There were famous admirers of Ferdinand: Thomas Mann, H. G. Wells, Mahandas Gandhi, and Franklin Roosevelt, whom Lawson, citing the virtues of private enterprise, disliked. (When he once planned a series "giving the real lowdown on various historical characters," he wished he "might live long enough to see FDR in proper perspective. The present seems distinctly cockeyed" [quoted in Jones, 52].) The book was used by political activists, and both Franklin Roosevelt and Stalin appeared in political cartoons as the passive bull. Some judged it to be pro-Franco, others anti-Franco; in any case it was banned in Spain until Franco's death, although it was available in Stalinist Poland—the only American children's book in that country at the time. And of course the book had its detractors: the *Cleveland Plain Dealer* argued that the book corrupted the youth of America. Hitler burned it in Nazi Germany, claiming that it was "degenerate democratic propaganda."

But these detractors were answered. To the *Cleveland Plain Dealer,* the *New York Times* replied that "there are those who love Ferdinand for his own sake, and don't care whether he is a Nazi or a Communist, so long as he is true to himself." And for Nazi Germany, the reply was more telling. After the fall of Berlin, 30,000 copies were distributed to the children of that city as a mission of peace (Hearn, 22). Leaf's own response affirmed the peace and joy at the center of the book: "I have been accused of defending or attacking practically every 'ism' that has popped up in the last few years. As far as I am concerned, there is one story there—the words are simple and quite short. They try to make sense and if there is a message in them, as many people seem to want, it is Ferdinand's message, not mine—get it from him according to your need" (quoted in Leaf, 33). Later, though, Leaf did seem to suggest that *The Story of Ferdinand* did have a message: "It was propaganda all right, but propaganda for laughter only. . . . If the book fails to make you chuckle, there is no excuse for its existence, as far as I'm concerned" (quoted in Hearn, 22). Fifteen years later this light aspect of the story was clearly on the mind of Ernest Hemingway, who opened his fable "The Faithful Bull" with a recognizable allusion: "One time there was a bull and his name was not Ferdinand and he cared nothing for flowers. He loved to fight and he fought with all the other bulls of his own age, or any age, and he was a champion."[14] The illustration for the story, first published in 1951 in *Holiday* magazine, depicts a large black bull pointedly ignoring a flower.

As Marie Lawson had observed, *The Story of Ferdinand* was fortuitous, but not only in itself; it led to a series of successful collaborations and to some of Lawson's most memorable work. Lawson would illustrate three more Leaf books: *Wee Gillis* in 1938 and *Aesop's Fables* and *The Story of Simpson and Sampson* in 1941. Nineteen thirty-eight would also see what is, after *The Story of Ferdinand,* perhaps Lawson's best-known collaborative work: Richard and Florence Atwater's *Mr. Popper's Penguins.* Children's books were indeed taking up more of his time. He had found a profession. By the late 1930s he had abandoned his commercial work; in 1937 he drew several Ruppert Beer ads that were noted in the *Creative Artist* (Gardner, 9). Other than these drawings, he worked exclusively in children's literature.

In 1938 Lawson changed direction yet again. Up until this time he had illustrated only, but with *Ben and Me* (1939) he developed his first text as a children's writer. Helen Jones, his editor at Little, Brown, had suggested the idea of a story about a famous historical character and his pet. Lawson made a list, then settled on Benjamin Franklin. The idea of this pairing—a historical figure with a fantasy pet—was suited to Lawson's skills as well as his interests. Many of his books, beginning with his collaboration with Arthur Mason, had dealt with fantasy elements, and here he was simply using that element in a historical setting. But it is noteworthy in this first written text of Lawson's that he choose the subject for its illustrative qualities. In October 1938 he wrote the art director at Little, Brown that "I have been thinking over the Famous person and his pet idea and have sort of boiled it down to one that I think ought to work out very well—it certainly would be a grand opportunity for drawings" (quoted in Jones, 73).

This happy discovery of a form and a genre, what Lawson called his "cock-eyed histories," led to three additional books along the same lines: *I Discover Columbus* (1941), *Mr. Revere and I* (1953), and *Captain Kidd's Cat* (1956). Lawson had settled on Paul Revere for his third book in the series by July of 1941, but it was delayed for a decade by both other commissions and a poor market reception for *I Discover Columbus*. In December 1951 he wrote to Little, Brown that he had "started on a new opus, about Paul Revere, as written by his horse."[15] Work on *Captain Kidd's Cat* started three years later, as Lawson began a year of research. He decided to use his own cat as a model for McDermot, the narrator: "Did you know that Captain Kidd's cat, Gallagher, wore a small gold ring set with a ruby in his left ear? . . . [I] am doing some research and taking photographs of our Blitzkrieg who, whether he likes it or not, is gong to be Kidd's cat."[16]

The late 1930s saw Lawson getting significant recognition for his work in children's literature. In 1938 he won the Caldecott Honor for his illustration of Helen Dean Fish's *Four and Twenty Blackbirds*; in 1939 he won the Caldecott Honor again for his illustration of Munro Leaf's *Wee Gillis,* and *Mr. Popper's Penguins* won a Newbery Honor. In 1941 Lawson won the Caldecott Medal itself for *They Were Strong and Good,* a picturebook that explored three generations of his own family. Lawson saw in his family a prototype: theirs was the story of all American families—simple, ordinary people who worked hard and were strong and good and who built a country out of a wilderness. The goal of the book was very explicit: to foster responsibility for and pride in America.

In his Caldecott award acceptance speech, Lawson argued that children are more imaginative than adults and suggested that their vulnerability led the children's book author to a certain kind of responsibility: "They are too close to the everlasting truth from which they have sprung. They have not yet been educated or 'guided' or 'molded' into the awful rules of grownupness. They are, for a pitifully few short years, honest and sincere, clear-eyed and open-minded. To give them anything less than the utmost that we possess of frankness, honesty and sincerity is, to my mind, the lowest possible crime" ("Caldecott," 275).

Lawson would deal with this romantic vision of childhood again in *At That Time,* but his aversion to deliberate molding of a child's mind and taste recalls his mother's willingness to expose him to art and literature without prejudgment. He concluded his speech with a return to this theme: "They will do their own choosing, they will do their own selecting, and what they choose will be honest and of good repute" ("Caldecott," 284). This was a theme much on Lawson's mind in the beginning of the 1940s. Six months before his Caldecott acceptance he had published "Make Me a Child Again" in *Horn Book,* in which he argued for the perceptive qualities of his child readers. Rejecting the notion of a "children's illustrator," he argued against "writing down" to children and said that he saw no difference between his early work and his work in children's literature, except that "their approval of what they like is thorough and honest and wholehearted. And what they do not like they can ignore with an indifference that is devastating" ("Make Me," 449).

The early 1940s saw the emergence of a golden age in children's literature. New illustrators such as Marcia Brown, Virginia Lee Burton, Robert McCloskey, William Pène du Bois, Roger Duvoisin, Marie Hall Ets, Leo Politi, Louis Slobodkin, Leonard Weisgard, and Holling C. Holling began to establish themselves. Lawson was a part of this surge, and part of the energy that impelled it was the coming war. Lawson followed *They Were Strong and Good* with a volume even more explicitly patriotic: *Watchwords of Liberty* (1943). It was a collection (a "pageant" as Lawson termed it) of well-known American phrases—phrases that had been uttered at defining moments in American history. Throughout 1942 he worked on *Watchwords of Liberty,* finally concluding in September of that year that this was "rather a magnum opus, of much more importance than any book that I have done yet."[17] He was wrong about that; this would not be a lasting book, despite a 1957 reprint, but it does suggest his large thematic interest in the vision of the American spirit of independence.

After *Ben and Me,* Lawson began a series of 20 books that he both wrote and illustrated from 1939 until his death 18 years later. He experimented with genres, developing historical fantasies, patriotic anthologies, folk tales, whimsical nonsense stories, and animal fantasies. It was this last category that led to his two most famous novels: *Rabbit Hill* and *The Tough Winter.* Those began as something quite different from animal fantasies, however. Little, Brown commissioned from Lawson a book about a city dweller who has to get used to the trials of country life; this would eventually turn into *Country Colic* (1944). But as Lawson wrote and interjected the rabbits that he found around his own home, he became more and more interested in rabbits themselves. As he wrote about the difficulties of gardening, of skunks upsetting the garbage and foxes killing off the chickens and leaky roofs and flooded cellars, he found himself becoming more interested in the stories of the animals than of the trials they caused: "The first thing I knew the little animals had taken over the book entirely and were writing their own story."[18] He saw the book as particularly appropriate to children: "I do think it has that cozy-home and home-life atmosphere the children love in stories of animals, also very definite characters which they also love."[19]

And as with *The Story of Ferdinand,* Little, Brown made the wrong decision. When the book they had commissioned did not come in, Robert L. Scaife, an editor at Little, Brown, rejected *Rabbit Hill.* May Massee accepted it immediately for Viking, however. Later, Scaife would write to Lawson, congratulating him on the book and concluding that the only blemish was the imprint (Gardner, 11).

The years following *Rabbit Hill* saw Lawson continuing the patterns that he had established in the late 1930s and early 1940s. He published three more fantasy books centering on the rabbits of his home: *Robbut: A Tale of Tails* (1948), a book that allowed him his last use of the wee little men that had begun his career; *Edward, Hoppy and Joe* (1952); and *The Tough Winter* (1954), the sequel to *Rabbit Hill.* He published the next three "cock-eyed" histories. He continued the strain of autobiography he had begun in *They Were Strong and Good* with *At That Time* (1947), a book Lawson called "a study of childhood, based somewhat on my own, written for adults" (quoted in Jones, 92). And he continued his celebration of America in *The Great Wheel* (1957).

But Lawson, who had moved from one artistic form to another all his life, added one more genre: whimsical and comic fantasies. In a sense here he was going back to his roots as an illustrator, but now he began to write as well, placing his fantasies not in the far-away, once-upon-a-time lands he had illustrated, but in the contemporary world. This series began with *Mr. Wilmer* in 1945, and over the next six years Lawson produced four more: *Mr. Twigg's Mistake* (1947), *The Fabulous Flight* (1949), *Smeller Martin* (1950), and *McWhinney's Jaunt* (1951).

His productivity remained astonishingly high, his demands on himself unremitting throughout the 1950s, when he was focusing on his historical fantasies. He had achieved the "Utopia" that he said he wanted—to be able to live on the royalties of a perpetually selling book—and he was free to abandon all illustration but that of his own writing. Nevertheless, he continued to illustrate the occasional textbook and to work eight or nine hours every day of the year, Sundays and holidays notwithstanding, with only very brief breaks for gardening or for short trips to Nantucket, the Berkshires, or Virginia between books. But, as his editor at Little, Brown remembers, even these would be shortened by his impatience to begin a new job (Jones, 110).

In 1956 Marie died; they had been married for 34 years, the entire time that Lawson had worked as a children's illustrator. Lawson was to outlive her by only a year. He died suddenly in the spring while working on the drawings for a short, whimsical book he had tentatively entitled *Why Bats Are*. He did not live to see the final production of his last book, *The Great Wheel* (1957).

Jennie D. Lindquist, the editor of *Horn Book,* began the August 1957 issue with a sober memorial to "The Master of Rabbit Hill": "It is sad to think that there will be no more books from the pen of this gifted author-artist, but good indeed to know that those he had written and illustrated will live for generations."[20] Lawson left behind him a legacy: *The Story of Ferdinand, Mr. Popper's Penguins, Rabbit Hill, The Tough Winter, Ben and Me.* As his other books pass into the hands of antiquarian book collectors, these five will continue to pass into the hands of children.

Chapter Two

The American Experience

Robert Lawson was always at the task of writing about the American experience. This is true of his historical fantasies, where he focuses on distinctly American figures. In such books as *The Great Wheel* (1957) he focuses on distinctly American institutions; in *Watchwords of Liberty* (1943) he focuses on distinctly American texts. All are different aspects of Lawson's vision of the American experience. As expressed in *They Were Strong and Good* (1940), the American experience is one of anonymous individuals—anonymous outside their own families—who are marked by physical and moral courage.

They Were Strong and Good

They Were Strong and Good was published in 1940, a time when Americans were looking across both oceans and seeing a world coming to pieces. The Old World seemed to have lost the ethical direction and vitality of the New, and there was a sense abroad that the American pioneer spirit marked the difference. And these were pioneers who, although anonymous, established a nation that was to supersede the Old World not only because of its youth but because of its moral impetus.

Lawson's foreword suggests not only this interest in the physical and moral qualities of his ancestors, but his autobiographical method: he will use this work to talk about the larger American experience. "Most of [this story]," he writes, "I heard as a little boy, so there may be many mistakes; perhaps I have forgotten or mixed up some of the events and people. But that does not really matter, for this is not alone the story of my parents and grandparents, it is the story of the parents and grandparents of most of us who call ourselves Americans." The story, then, is mythic; Lawson is not as concerned with the specifics as he is with the larger meanings that the story will generate. And he is quite explicit about the meaning of the myth: "None of them were great or famous, but they were strong and good. They worked hard and had many children. They all helped to make the United States the great nation that it now is." So individual experience leads to the larger, communal experience—to, in fact, a meaning that allows the past to inform the present. For Lawson, this meaning is such an important part of the book that he concludes the foreword with a challenge to the reader: "Let us be proud of them and guard well the heritage they have left us." With this challenge, the book becomes more than a series of intriguing vignettes, more than the story of one family; it becomes an archetypal American story.

Lawson tells the tale of his own grandparents and parents, following them in short, vividly illustrated stories that merge into one another as the characters become acquainted. His mother's father was a Scottish sea captain who sailed to South America, buying sugarcane and panama hats; he met Lawson's mother's mother while supplying his ship with the produce that she and her father had brought to the market from their farm in New Jersey. They married, and because she did not like the sea and he had grown tired of it, they moved to Minnesota, where "they worked very hard and were strong and good" and "they had many children." One of those children was Lawson's mother, who remembers Indians, wild Saturday nights when the lumberjacks came into town, and the quiet convent where she learned to take the honeycomb from beehives without being stung.

Lawson's father's father was a fighter: first he had fought in the Seminole War, and then he went from town to town fighting Satan with hellfire sermons. His father's mother thought that he fought Satan very well, and so she married him: "They worked hard and were strong and good." One of their children was Lawson's father, and most of the book is given over to his tale. When his father went away to fight the Yankees instead of Satan, Lawson's father stayed home, itching to be in the war. With gold strapped around his middle, he rode a fine horse to safety from the Yankees and deserters in the countryside. Soon after that he signed on with General Joseph E. Johnston and became the guidon bearer, the boy who marked the spot where the cannon were to be placed. But there were, as the war drew on, fewer and fewer cannon, and finally he was wounded, forced to retreat, and then return home, defeated. His father had gone back to fighting Satan, but his old life was gone. Lawson's father went to New York, where his southern accent and limp made him an object of scorn, except to a lady who had come all the way from Minnesota to visit in New York: "So they were married. They worked hard and were strong and good. They had many children and one of them happened to be ME."

The book concludes with a return to the challenge that had ended the foreword: "I am proud of my mother and my father and of their mothers and fathers. And I am proud of the country that they helped to build." Thus the individual story merges into the mythic. His grandparents and parents are part of Indian wars, the Civil War, the movement west, the vital mercantile fleet—all mythic parts of American history.

The reviews for *They Were Strong and Good* focused quite specifically on this mythic quality; most commented on its distinctly American sense. "Through simple text and a great many excellent illustrations, Robert Lawson has passed on to us the impressions he gained of his forebears during childhood. The result is an exceptionally acceptable book for the younger children about the kind of people who helped to make the United States a great nation," wrote J. E. Stromdahl in *Library Journal*.[1] "In the few words between his very worth while drawings, Mr. Lawson conjures a whole American saga," suggested the reviewer of *Catholic World*.[2] The *Horn Book* review by A. M. Jordan connected the individual and communal experience: "the book [is] a bit of social history out of the family album."[3] The reviewer for the *Christian Science Monitor* took up the concluding challenge of the foreword: "This artist, whose work is always distinguished, has given to young Americans and their elders, not only a beautiful picture book but a timely reminder that they too must be 'strong and good'; must give their best to their country and keep America strong and free."[4] A. T. Eaton, writing in the *New York Times Book Review*, agreed: "Of all the books designed to teach boys and girls the meaning of democracy and to encourage patriotism that are being hurried to press today, this one is likely to make the deepest impression on children."[5]

Half a century later it is perhaps not this quality that is most memorable about this, Lawson's only Caldecott-winning book. What remains striking about *They Were Strong and Good* is the function of the illustrations. They are, first, striking in their narrative quality. The text of *They Were Strong and Good* is sparse, and little of it is given over to either characterization or establishing settings; these are the tasks of the illustrations almost entirely. The illustration of Lawson's grandfather leaving to fight the Yankees is particularly telling in this regard. The very moment of leavetaking has come. The boys are weeping, their hands to eyes that have turned away from the road. The grandmother, composed and resigned, has turned away; she will not weep; she will maintain a control that is essential for the family. The grandfather, uniformed and somewhat stern, looks down the road he will take; his rifle is already pointed in that direction. Although he has taken his first step down the road to war, his hand remains clasped to his wife's; the reluctance to leave one world and take up responsibility for another is evident. The plantation

FROM *THEY WERE STRONG AND GOOD* BY ROBERT LAWSON. COPYRIGHT 1940 BY ROBERT LAWSON, RENEWED (C) 1968 BY JOHN W. BOYD. USED BY PERMISSION OF VIKING PENGUIN, A DIVISION OF PENGUIN BOOKS USA INC.

setting, the pain of separation, the varying responses of the characters—all are told in the illustration. The text, however, indicates none of this: "When the Civil War began, my father's father quit fighting Satan and went off to fight the Yankees instead." None of the pathos is expressed; the tone remains distant and objective.

The investment of character is almost completely the role of the illustration; the text maintains this distance, this sense of the reporter. The
illustration of his mother's father on the deck of his vessel accompanies a
sparse test: "A great storm came on before they reached New York and
my mother's father had to stay on deck for two days and two nights."
Lawson uses the illustration to depict the danger and terror of the scene:
the seas like mountains, the deck completely covered with water so that
the ropes seem to spring down into nothing but water, the close-up of
the captain, his face filled with a sturdy command, his mouth open to
holler his orders; there is no sense of terror in his expression. When Lawson writes that his grandmother did not like sailing, he uses his illustration to explain why: she stands on tiptoe, leaning as far as she can over
the side of the ship. The serene poses of his grandmother as a young girl
in the convent, the glare of the fanatic on his grandfather's face as he
fights Satan, the yearning hopefulness of his father when he first meets
his mother—all this narrative and establishment of character is left to
the illustrations.

Nowhere is this narrative quality more evident than in the series of
five illustrations showing his father's involvement in the Civil War. They
begin with an illustration of the mule that is assigned to his father; the
text is, as usual, sparse: "It wasn't much of a mule, but my father wasn't
much of a man yet, so they got on fine." In fact, there is clearly real
affection between them: the boy reaches out to the muzzle of the mule,
which is as lanky and thin as the horse of the picadores in *The Story of
Ferdinand.* Behind him, three shadowy soldiers look on, laughing, as if
finding the connection of the lanky boy with the lanky mule funny. But
the following illustration shows no humor; Lawson's father is given the
task of guidon bearer: he is to hold the flag to mark the spot where the
cannon are to be placed. He sits astride his mule, and there is nothing
short of dignity about him. The mule stands straight, his neck arched;
the boy sits up straight, holding the guidon absolutely vertical. In fact,
the strong sense of vertical line dominates this illustration, contrasting
with the random line of the ground beneath them.

In the third illustration, the mule is gone, taken by the captain when
his horse is killed. But the boy, standing now, remains absolutely
straight. The flag, ragged and battered, is still in the center of the illustration. This time the strong vertical line of the boy and his flag are con-
trasted by the horizontal movement of the troops fleeing from the battle. (The boy stands rigidly looking toward it.) The bayonets are angled
randomly—another contrast—and the soldiers who look at the boy are

no longer laughing; there is respect in their eyes. In the fourth illustration the horizontal movement of the retreat continues, but now the vertical line is diminished. The boy has been wounded and uses the flagpole for a crutch; it is held at a slight angle, and the boy is hunched over as he tries to walk. In the final illustration of the sequence, the pole is now just a cane; the boy walks down a street of devastated buildings, the vertical lines supplied by a blasted tree and the chimneys that still stand. The boy is diminished in the picture, too, although he remains at the center, trying to cope with the loss. And the loss is a tremendous one, though again the poignancy of the loss is not stressed at all in the text: "By the time my father's leg was well the Yankees had won the war, so he walked back to Alabama. His father had quit fighting Yankees and had gone back to fighting Satan. The store had been burned down and there was no work, and Numa Pompilius and Sextus Hostilius [his two hunting dogs] and Dick [his slave and hunting companion] were all gone too."

The power of this story is conveyed almost exclusively in the illustrations; the text takes on the objective voice of the historian; the illustrations depict the poignancy of the family member retelling an old story. The enormous dignity of the young boy, the courage in the face of disaster, the loss of hope, and the final recognition of the disaster that had befallen him, mirror the larger story of the South in the Civil War. Both individual and communal stories merge here, and both are poignant because of the focus on the single individual.

The other striking quality of the illustrations in *They Were Strong and Good* is Lawson's fusion of word and illustration, allowing them to play back and forth on each other. This fusion is in part possible because of the strong narrative quality of the illustrations. In describing the city of his grandmother's youth, Lawson writes, "The City of Paterson stands there now and looks about like this—" The "about" suggests a kind of vagueness, but there is nothing vague about the accompanying illustration. The city straddles a river and seems to consist wholly of warehouses and factories that spew their effulgence as fast as they can into the water and air. In fact, the illustration is dominated by an array of smokestacks that fill the air with grainy soot.

The text that accompanies this disagreeable scene remains as objective and dispassionate as the rest of the text; it is left to the illustration to make the point that progress has ruined this city. But the text also sounds something like the text that might accompany a travelogue—an impression strengthened by the following page: "But in those days it looked more like this—" Here, too, is the fusion of text with illustration, as the eye is directed by the text to the illustration, and the meaning of the text is completely dependent on the reading of that illustration. Here the scene is idyllic, a strong contrast to the scene of the polluted city. The illustration emphasizes harmony and fecundity—as well as an ecological sense. A father and daughter stand in a farmyard, surrounded by hens, cows, geese, turkeys, and a wagon loaded with the produce of their garden. The barn is so filled that hay bursts from its loft. There is no ease here, but there is contentment—"they were strong and good."

This fusion of text and illustration is also part of the six portraits Lawson uses, those of his grandparents and parents. Each is preceded by a text that introduces them in the same voice as the travelogue, or as a speaker might introduce the pictures found in a family album—which, in a sense, is precisely what Lawson is doing. Writing of his paternal grandparents, Lawson uses a refrain that leads directly to the illustration of his father: "So they were married. They worked hard and were strong and good. They had many children and one of them was—" Here the text breaks off and is continued on the next page as the heading over the portrait of Lawson's father. The final effect, then, is of a seamless whole, with text and illustration working together and individually to tell the story. With *The Story of Ferdinand,* it is perhaps Lawson's finest work.

Watchwords of Liberty

Written midway through America's involvement in World War II, *Watchwords of Liberty: A Pageant of American Quotations* was meant to celebrate in very specific ways the triumph of American history, to celebrate America's fortitude, resolve, and courage: "Today more than five million young Americans stand armed and ready to uphold this pledge [of allegiance] that they made as children, stand ready to offer up their lives in defense of their flag and the Republic for which it stands," Lawson writes in a preface.[6] This is, in short, a book that comes very much out of World War II.

The book's structure is a simple one. Lawson quotes a well-known American phrase, accompanies it with an explanatory text, and supports it with an illustration. Sometimes these illustrations are portraitlike, as, for example, those of Benjamin Franklin or George Washington. Sometimes they are narrative in quality, as in that accompanying Emerson's poetic "shot heard 'round the world" that Lawson illustrates with a somewhat fanciful scene from the battle at Concord's Old North Bridge. And at times his illustrations are interpretive; the illustration accompanying Lincoln's famous "with malice toward none, with charity for all" inaugural speech shows Lincoln's reposed face as part of the American landscape, suggesting the permanence of his impact on this country.

The 57 texts that Lawson quotes reflect the predilections of 1943. There are no women in any of these pages, and only Booker T. Washington suggests the presence of the African-American culture. This is clearly an Anglo-Saxon world, where Lawson warns against excessive immigration and depicts races as distinctly "other." When describing the driving of the last spike on the continental railroad, Lawson writes that "there were wild-looking Irish laborers, a few soldiers, Chinese coolies in broad straw hats, and a scattering of blanketed Indians" (76). The illustrations show these groups—all separate—as standing quite apart from the august ceremonies, despite the fact that they are the ones who actually built the thing. All of this suggests that Lawson is a man writing in his own time, with its sensibilities.

The texts themselves, the pageant of them, illustrate Lawson's vision of what makes America great. There are, as one might expect, not a few texts that come out of American battles: "Don't fire until you see the whites of their eyes" from Bunker Hill; "I have not yet begun to fight" from John Paul Jones; "I shall never surrender nor retreat" from the Alamo; "There is Jackson, standing like a stone-wall" from the first battle of Bull Run; "You may fire when ready, Gridley" from the Spanish-American War; "Sighted sub—sank same" from the opening days of America's involvement in World War II. A number of the texts celebrate American inventions, such as Thomas Edison's "There is no substitute for hard work," Samuel Morse's "What hath God wrought?" and Alexander Graham Bell's "Mr. Watson, come here; I want you." Some celebrate America's foundation in the principles of liberty, such as James Otis's "Taxation without representation is tyranny," Patrick Henry's "Give me liberty, or give me death!," and Thomas Jefferson's "We hold those truths to be self-evident." In fact, political oratory is much celebrated in this pageant, including memorable phrases such as William Jennings Bryan's "cross of gold," Theodore Roosevelt's "speak softly and carry a big stick," and Franklin Roosevelt's "the only thing we have to fear is fear itself."

Although the book's title suggests its orientation, not all of the texts that Lawson includes would today be remembered as "watchwords of liberty." James Henry Hammond's "Cotton is King" declaration in 1858

might not fit here today, nor perhaps would Theodore Roosevelt's jingo-
istic "There is room here for only 100 percent Americanism." But even
as he includes these texts, Lawson seems aware of their problematic
nature. He includes, for example, Stephen Decatur's "Our country, right
or wrong," but questions the legitimacy of this sentiment and even
draws attention away from the speech to the speaker. Those words,
Lawson writes, "live in every American's memory, but there has always
been some question as to whether such blind loyalty to country is
morally proper. . . . Whether or not we question the correctness of his
words, we can never forget the glory of his deeds" (38). Lawson's pointing is to the heroism rather than the jingoism.

The pageant of quotations is framed by a passage from *Mourt's Relation* on the voyage of the *Mayflower:* "So they commited them selves to
the will of God and resolved to proseede." Lawson's admiration for their
resolve is evident: "They were leaving forever homes, friends, and kindred, comforts, trades, civilization, all that men hold dear. Yet with a
high courage and steadfast purpose, turning their backs on all these
things, faces toward the sunset"—and here Lawson quotes again the
words from *Mourt's Relation*. These words become an underpinning for
the entire book, as in their own way, all of the texts suggest this resolve
to proceed. The book, in fact, concludes with those same words, used in
conjunction with a text from Franklin Roosevelt: "The heart of this
nation is sound—the spirit of this nation is strong—the faith of this
nation is eternal," lines spoken in 1943, just six months before the
book's publication.

Lawson's commentaries on the texts are marked by a somewhat
restrained exuberance, a kind of subdued bursting of buttons. To the text
"Hold the fort; I am coming," wired from William Sherman to a besieged
commander, Lawson notes that by the time Sherman arrived, General
Corse "had lost one third of his men, a cheekbone and one ear, but was
still full of fight" (58). At times this exuberance bursts through and
becomes immoderate, particularly in the battlecry texts: "Remember the
Alamo!" "Remember the Maine!" "Remember Pearl Harbor!" When Lawson comments about the Alamo, he speaks of the "cringing, bedraggled
Santa Anna," who was dragged in front of Sam Houston, "a captive" (50).
His comments on Pearl Harbor begin with a comment on how the day
will live "bitterly in the hearts of Americans" and "stand as a supreme
example of a nation's infamy" (109). But his anger is not reserved for the
Japanese alone: "We will remember the criminally careless leadership
which allowed this treacherous attack to succeed with such ease" (109).

At times Lawson's commentary has the voice of historical objectivity, as in his description of the popular "Go west, young man," which he attributes to a John Babsone Lane Soule rather than to Horace Greeley (74). But objectivity is not at all the effect for which Lawson is searching. Although he uses the metaphor of a pageant, a more appropriate metaphor might be a narrative, for here is history as story, and it is the same story as his Caldecott-winning book: this is a story about those who are strong and good. This means that Lawson, like any teller of stories, is not averse to using narrative effects to achieve his purpose. In writing of the death of Nathan Hale, Lawson juxtaposes images to suggest the poignancy of early death: "With the dishonoring noose dangling, young Nathan Hale looked his last on the bright gold leaves of early autumn, gazed on the brilliant blue sky of his native land and spoke the words forever engraved on the shield of America's honor" (20). In describing the opening of the Revolution, Lawson dramatically shifts his narrative stance by merging his audiences, bringing together the experience of the revolutionaries with that of the reader: "Down came the lions and unicorns, the gilded coats of arms. Into the fires with them—and the bright flames proclaimed Liberty throughout the land" (12). In chronicling the end of the Civil War, Lawson turns to metaphor, mixed though it might be: "Clearly the Confederacy was dying and like eager buzzards the apostles of hate and venom, of greed and vengeance, were gathering for the feast" (69). In each case Lawson is the storyteller using his literary technique to embellish the story of America.

In 1957 Lawson published a new edition of *Watchwords of Liberty* that is virtually identical to the 1943 version. The paragraph dealing with the present circumstances of World War II is dropped from the preface. The opening paragraph about the war in Europe is dropped from the foreword. Of the 57 quotations, only one is changed, and the change reflects the changed time. Where in 1943 Lawson includes a Franklin Roosevelt text to suggest the country's fortitude during the war, now he includes John Philpot Curran's "Eternal vigilance is the price of liberty," and Lawson's commentary in this cold war age warns of foreign enemies, internal subversion, and "unscrupulous politicians who have sought to gain popularity among certain segments of our people by tampering with or circumventing the law of our land."[7] One would be hard-pressed not to identify that last with Joseph McCarthy. In concluding his book with the call to eternal vigilance, he loses the symmetrical frame he had established in the first edition and crafts a book suited to the peculiar fears of his time.

Chapter Three
The Historical Fantasies

J. R. R. Tolkien has suggested that fantasy concerns the creation of an "other" world, a secondary world that has its own internal integrity and reference. This is certainly the dominant understanding of fantasy in the late twentieth century. It is, however, not the only understanding, and between 1939 and 1956 Robert Lawson wrote four novels in which he combined fantasy with historical fiction. Other than *Rabbit Hill* and *A Tough Winter,* these four represent some of his most accomplished writing.

The most renowned of these historical fantasies is *Ben and Me,* its fame secured not only through the text but through the good auspices of a Disney film version. Here a mouse retells the story of Benjamin Franklin, changing conventionally understood history to show that Franklin's accomplishments were really those of the mouse narrator. Similar changes dominate *I Discover Columbus,* in which a parrot leads Columbus to the New World (actually the parrot's home); *Captain Kidd's Cat;* and *Mr. Revere and I,* in which a horse tells Paul Revere's story. The titles of three of the books suggest what is true of all: the animal narrator dominates; he is the "I" and the "Me" of the titles, out to set things right. Thus the gentle fantasy of the books.

The books represent a rather curious fusion, one that is maintained in their illustrations. On the one hand they are clearly fantasies, in which animals speak and fantastic things happen in generally humorous ways. The illustrations reflect this in their typical Lawson exaggeration. On the other hand, however, these books do follow fairly closely the actual careers of Franklin, Revere, Captain Kidd, and Columbus, with some attempt to accurately reproduce historical episodes.

What brings these two disparate genres together is in fact the narrator, who strides across both with a scornful and sometimes even cynical vision of how history has gone awry: "I could tell you who really discovered the Americas, I could tell,"[1] exclaims the furious parrot Aurelio in *I Discover Columbus,* and he could speak for all of these narrators. They can and will tell what really happened. Thus history is slanted and turned into fantasy in Lawson's hands, so that frequently we see the narrator more than the action itself.

This perspective is particularly emphasized on the cover of *I Discover Columbus*. Here Columbus peers through his telescope, gaping in open-mouthed wonder at what he sees. But in fact Aurelio the parrot is perched on the telescope and leans over, so that all Columbus can see must be seen through the interposition of the parrot. The reader is in much the same position as the hapless Columbus; everything will come through the perspective of the animal narrator.

Perhaps another way of looking at these novels, however, is to consider the ways in which they recast history so that it comes from the perspective of a child. Instead of the Mount Rushmore–caliber figures that dominate history books, Lawson presents characters who would be much more real to a child audience. His characters are comic, a bit bumbling, prone to error, willing to take chances when encouraged, willing to make and accept mistakes, and often in positions where others lord their huge selves over them. In fact, as this description suggests, they are often like children, in terms of both their childlike natures and their situations. Perhaps Lawson may be faulted for rarely using a child protagonist, but in reading these four novels, one sees that he is not far away from such a protagonist.

Ben and Me

Much of the comedy of *Ben and Me* (1939), which was published as Europe was slouching toward war, is centered on the practical-minded mouse narrator, Amos, and his undercutting of the great Benjamin Franklin. But much of the book's comedy also lies with the undercutting of historical understandings; in fact, the two sources are not much different. For example, Amos tells a new tale of the writing of the Declaration of Independence. When a committee of five comes together in Philadelphia to write the document, Thomas Jefferson brings with him a red-haired mouse known as Red Jefferson. He is a firebrand and radical, but a good writer. Convincing all of the local mice that they have been villainously abused by man, he sets out to write a document asserting their freedom from this domination: "When in the course of human events it becomes necessary for a mouse to dissolve the bands which have linked him to his master,"[2] the document begins. Amos reads the document to Ben Franklin, who has returned from one of his committee meetings quite discouraged. Enthused, Ben copies the document and presents it to the full congress, which adopts it as the Declaration of Independence. Here a mouse is given a play in extraordinarily large

events; he influences Ben and his role as a diplomat, and he helps
Franklin borrow the money from France necessary to fund the American
Revolution. The shift in perspective, the shift in principal actors, and the
shift in anticipated tone all add to the humor Lawson is using.

The book opens with Amos's resolve to set the record straight on
Franklin's accomplishments, and he pictures himself as the eldest of a
family of 26. He sets out to find his way in the world and comes upon
Franklin, struggling to warm his room with a smoking fire. Amos suggests a new contraption, something in the middle of the room that will
warm the entire area. "Ben was a fair terror for work, once he was interested" (13), Amos points out, and soon Ben has put together what
Amos dubs the Franklin stove, letting him have all the credit.

Amos and Ben realize the usefulness of their collaboration and draw
up a bargain that both sign; Amos is to advise Ben, while Ben is to provide food twice a week to Amos's family. The partnership leads to a close
friendship. Amos accompanies Ben on his swimming ventures; he assists
him (a bit disastrously) in his printing shop, although he scoffs at the
eternal maxims; and he watches as Ben begins his experiments with
electricity. Here, however, he is put off and unwilling to participate. But
Ben finds his assistance invaluable, and finally is able to trap Amos in a
kite during a thunderstorm, intending to find out if lightning is composed of electricity. This leads to a rift, repaired only by Ben's promises
to cease dabbling in electrical experiments.

When relations are strained between England and its colonies, Ben
rushes off to England—unaccompanied by Amos, as he has installed a
lightning rod on the mast of the ship. When he returns, Amos con-
tributes to the war effort as best he can, by helping Ben write the Declaration of Independence and then, in France, subverting the plots of
those who wish to harm Franklin's mission. Amos soon grows tired of
France, however, particularly as Ben is pampered by the court of Louis
XVI. Amos's attention is diverted from his boredom, however, when he
comes upon a story that leads him to reenact on a mouse scale the war
that the colonies have so recently won.

Sophie, a white mouse, has been separated from her family. Her husband was betrayed by a conspiracy and forced into exile in America.
Sophie was forced to flee Versailles, leaving her seven children captive
beneath the thrones. When Amos resolves to help, he frames the task in
familiar terms: " 'Fear not, Madame,' I said. 'To a true son of Liberty and
Justice, such a task is a mere nothing' " (83). Amos enlists the aid of Red
Jefferson, recently arrived with Thomas Jefferson, the first American

ambassador to France. Together they gather mice from the various national embassies, as well as mice from the streets of Paris and from the American fleet.

Ben, meanwhile, is ignorant of those preparations, too pleased with his reception in Paris and enjoying his popularity. Amos resolves to make his attack on the very night that a ball is to be held in Franklin's honor; it is to mark the end of Franklin's popularity. The mice hide all over Ben, and at Amos's signal, the mice leap off him and rush the throne. They attack the mice guarding the captives, but much of the army deserts to attack the lavish refreshments. Just when the battle seems to be turning against Amos, the mice from the American fleet appear:

> Through the window they came piling—the sailor rats of John Paul Jones! Fifty fighting Yankees! LAFAYETTE, WE ARE HERE!
> Flashing cutlasses and flailing handspikes drove through the throng. The white mice fled like snowflakes before a wind. In no time the cage was captured, the door demolished and Sophie's children brought forth, free mice! (101)

The language here suggests that Amos has done for France what France has done for America. The exclamation, "Lafayette, we are here!" echoes General Pershing's line at Lafayette's tomb at the opening of World War I. At the same time, however, Amos has humiliated and affrighted yet another decadent monarchy.

Ben, not being welcome at Versailles after this, heads back to Philadelphia, a hero, carrying Sophie and her children back to her husband—although he seems unaware of this. Ben is honored, just as he wished: "Our reception was everything that even Ben could have hoped for. There were salutes of cannon and firearms, there were delegations from Congress and a message from General Washington. The Mayor, the City Council and the First Volunteer Fire Brigade were all present, dressed in their best uniforms. There were floats, bands and a parade" (105). Ben is of course right at the center of this, honored here as he had been in Paris. The accompanying illustration shows him collared by a wreath of flowers. Crowds are lined up to see him, shooting off pistols and tossing their hats. Flags billow over him as bouquets are tossed, and Franklin beams. Almost unseen are the mice looking out from the beaver hats (104).

And this is apparently exactly how Amos wants things. He settles down with his family, surrounded by brothers and sisters and nieces and nephews. While other homes are busy raising families, and while Sophie's home becomes a brilliant social center, Amos placidly grows old: "I found more and more pleasure in staying quietly at home where I could enjoy the company of Sophie's children" (107), Amos suggests. He even withdraws from the still busy affairs of Franklin. When Amos and the other mice band together to give Franklin a fine new hat, Franklin frets because there is no place in it for Amos to ride. Amos tells him that he is 81, old enough to be on his own, and yet "you know that I'll always be here in the old fur cap, hanging on the bedpost, if you really need me" (113). And Amos curls into the old beaver hat and falls asleep, much like McDermot in the conclusion of *Captain Kidd's Cat.*

Like the other three historical fantasies, *Ben and Me* opens with a foreword that makes a pretense of establishing credibility. The book, it seems, is actually a manuscript discovered by workmen who are renovating an old Philadelphia house. To verify its authenticity, the manuscript is sent to Brownsonian Institute; to verify the nature of the writer, it is sent to the National Museum of Natural History. The suggestion here is that the manuscript has credibility—once, that is, the reader has made the leap from disbelief into fantasy. And Lawson, who appears quite clearly as the narrator in this foreword, goes further into his fantasy by noting the possible discrepancies between the conventional accounts of Franklin's career and that of Amos the mouse: "I am aware that his account of Franklin's career differs in many respects from the accounts of later historians. This I cannot explain but it seems reasonable to believe that statements made by one who lives on terms of such intimacy with this great man should be more trustworthy than those written by later scholars" (vii).

Ben and Me does more than allow readers a new perception of Franklin; it tells the story of Amos as he is caught up in the events of Franklin's career. This is emphasized even in the typography of the cover and title page, where "ME" appears much larger than "BEN." But this focus is also developed in the character of Amos, for he is the one who keeps the reader's attention. The book never strays from his activities. He is out to tell the real story of Franklin's accomplishments, but he is also eager to tell his own tale even when he veers from Franklin's career, as he does during their time in France together.

All of the narrators of Lawson's historical fantasies are distinctive: Aurelio is bitter; McDermot is saddened and eager for rest. Amos is Lawson's most successful narrator because he combines activity with perception. Aurelio is one who spurs action; McDermot is one who observes. But Amos does both. Perhaps he is able to do this because he comes upon Franklin not, as do Aurelio and McDermot, at the beginning of their significant careers but when Franklin is already established as a famous figure. What Amos does through his narration is to undercut the source of that fame. This comes about not only as Amos shows that he is himself responsible for many of Franklin's accomplishments but when he pictures Franklin as a lovable though vain and somewhat ridiculous figure. These two prongs of Amos's depiction dominate the narrative.

Both of these prongs are evident in Amos's first encounter with Franklin. When they meet, Ben is trying to warm his room through a fireplace, but Amos points out that most of the heat goes up the chimney and that no one can get around the stove. He advises Franklin to move the fire into the middle of the room, put iron around it, and use a pipe for the smoke. Franklin is enthused and instantly runs downstairs and begins to build what would become the Franklin stove. Franklin's pronouncement: "We've done it." Amos's reply: "Thanks for the WE. . . . I'll remember it" (16). The other prong is also part of this episode, for Franklin does seem ridiculous. He is unable to solve the most minor problem with the stove; for example, he cannot understand why it will not burn through the floor. He builds the stove out of what Amos calls junk, dropping nuts and screws and tools and his glasses, which Amos retrieves for him. The illustration shows him surrounded by a mess of tools, standing back to proudly survey his creation. But the stove itself is pictured as ridiculously hung together, the pipe and sides battered and dented, the whole thing hanging together, barely, with the help of twisted wires. Franklin's pride and cockiness is hardly justified, so that his stance makes him look ridiculous.

Although not always combined, these two prongs continue throughout the narrative. It is Amos who—sometimes unwittingly—is responsible for many of Franklin's discoveries about electricity. It is Amos who conceives of lightning rods and who is responsible for the Declaration of Independence, for Franklin's success and safety at the French court, for his heroic status back in Philadelphia. Riding inside Franklin's beaver cap, Amos serves as a guide and confidant; Franklin seems insecure without him.

And Amos clearly cares for Ben, just as McDermot cares for Kidd. Ben may be silly and ridiculous, but Amos's intention to help comes out of a real concern for Franklin and for his country—which is not something that the practical-minded Amos will articulate. Amos is Lawson's depiction of the shrewd Yankee. He dreams up a business partnership with Ben to ensure that his friendship will lead to food for his family. He at first agrees to accompany Franklin to England not just out of his love of country but also because "I understand that the English cheeses are of excellent quality" (64). Despite the cheese and patriotic yearnings, however, Amos refuses to go to England because of the lightning rods Franklin has mounted on the masts. Food and security are the practical qualities that drive Amos's judgment, according to his narrative, more than patriotic fervor.

Yet the illustrations belie this projected image of the mouse. When Amos is remarking on the superb quality of the wheat grown at Mount Vernon, the accompanying illustration shows nothing of this. He stands beside a pair of boots and the scabbard of Washington at attention. Amos is saluting and proudly holding an American flag, suggesting that despite his narrative, the primary effect of Washington is a stir to patriotism.

The same is true of Amos's relationship to Franklin. When Franklin mounts the lightning rods and Amos refuses to accompany him to England, it seems that he has broken with Franklin: "So I returned to the vestry and Ben sailed alone" (65), he writes, concluding this episode. But again the illustration suggests that there is no real break here. As the ship sails, Amos stands on a rock, his carpetbag beside him, watching and waving Ben to the horizon (64–65). Neither can possibly see the other, and for Amos there is clearly loss. But once again, this is something the Yankee mouse would never articulate in the narrative.

Perhaps this sense of fondness breaks through Amos's practicality at only one moment. When Ben is despondent over the loss of his reputation in France, Amos could have simply derided him for his vanity; it would have been consistent with his character. In fact, however, his response is quite different. He sets out to cheer the man: "But, Ben, . . . don't you realize that our own country of America is waiting to welcome you back as a hero?" (105). When Ben is at first unconvinced, Amos presses on: "Why, General Washington himself will probably be at the dock to meet us. There'll be bands, and parades—" (105). At the prospect of all this, Ben quickly cheers up. Amos's response suggests that his hard-nosed narrative, his insistence that he get the credit due him, is only one side of the relationship—the shrewd Yankee side. There is a deeper and more intimate side as well.

This episode suggests as well that Lawson is continuing to undercut his historical character—although the undercutting is gentle. He is not debunking a hero as much as humorously playing up some of that hero's weaknesses. Franklin is vain and proud at times, silly and naive in his enthusiasms, but he remains nonetheless a hero. This will be true of Paul Revere and William Kidd as well; it will not be true of Columbus, where the narration comes from a much more bitter narrator.

I Discover Columbus

I Discover Columbus (1941) may be the most problematic of Lawson's historical fantasies. *Ben and Me* had worked so well principally because of the engaging characters. Amos, while eager to set the record straight on Franklin's accomplishments, is essentially amiable and likable. Ben may be a bit slow and dim, but he is a man without guile and, in the end, has concerns larger than himself. He is truly interested in advancing science and establishing a new nation.

But in *I Discover Columbus,* the amiable narrator and bumbling but likable companion are gone. They are replaced by characters who are dominated by a meanness that not only diminishes them but distances them from the reader. Readers can identify with bumblers; they cannot feel much empathy for manipulators and graspers. Yet these are precisely the kinds of characters that Lawson creates for this novel. Aurelio, the narrating parrot, is simply mean; he seems to love nothing but his fruit, and when bad fortune besets him, he will manipulate others until he gets what he wants—his fruit and his homeland. Columbus himself begins as something of a bumbler, and if he was not shown to be terribly vain he might have been endearing in the opening pages. Instead, from vanity he progresses to greed, ambition, cowardice, and finally cruelty. It would be impossible to feel much for Columbus beyond what Aurelio feels: contempt. (That the other characters in the novel feel this too suggests that it is not merely a biased narrator who leads the reader to this position.)

But there are other novels that succeed despite a cast and narrator that strike the reader as unsavory, although these are rather rare in children's literature. More problematic about *I Discover Columbus* is the shallowly veiled meanness of the author himself. The portrayal of Columbus is unremittingly contemptuous. Columbus is not endearing in his bumbling or lovable in his silliness. He is dreadful through and through. The final double-page spread of Columbus sitting desolate under a canopy on the shore is not, as Aurelio seems moved to say, suggesting authorial pity; it seems to anticipate the final image of the mad Aguirre in Werner Herzog's 1972 film *Aguirre: The Wrath of God.*

But Columbus is not the only object of meanness. When Aurelio seeks to raise money for the expedition, he pawns two of Isabella's jewels to Don Issachar, who is the "least dishonest" (56) of any of the pawnbrokers. He is portrayed as the conventional Jewish moneylender, although Shylock himself is saintly compared to Don Issachar. He ignores the wonder of a talking bird to get at the stones; he is greedy, willing to steal, and well able to cheat. His hand, Aurelio suggests, is "not too clean" (59)—both in physical and moral terms.

Later, when Ferdinand interviews potential admirals, he comes upon "a mincing young man, gorgeously costumed" (65). His title, he tells Ferdinand, is an honorary one: "I have never seen the sea, but I have designed some of the loveliest gowns for Her Majesty, haven't I, Your Majesty?" (66). The ambiguous sexuality of the potential admiral is subject for ridicule. "Take it away" (66), says Ferdinand in dismissing him, his choice of pronoun indicative of his attitude.

The difficulty of these descriptions is that neither is at all necessary to the plot. Both Don Issachar and the admiral seem to put in cameo appearances for no other reason than to be caricatured and despised. While it is tempting to say that Lawson is only using these descriptions to suggest Aurelio's mean character, the fact that Lawson chooses to illustrate the two with grotesque exaggeration suggests that the difficulty lies with the author rather than the narrator. When Aurelio complains about the climate of Spain, that is legitimate. Where caricatured stereotypes are illustrated, that seems sheer ridicule.

It is the case that the story is principally Aurelio's, and the prime motive for events is his desire to return to his home in what would be eventually called the New World. He is blown to Spain by a terrible storm and finds himself in a Spanish monastery, weak and hungry, cold in this new climate, and unable to communicate with the monks. He is finally greeted by Christopher Columbus, a tattered yet vain man who is, at least, quick to establish a linguistic tie with the parrot. Over the next few weeks, Christopher teaches Aurelio Spanish; Aurelio, however, spends much of his time complaining about the cold weather.

Columbus has much to complain of, too; having spent an unhappy childhood as the son of a weaver in Genoa, he has wandered the countryside, looking for honor and wealth, and bestowing titles upon himself that no one else will recognize. Finally, poor and starving, he has come to the monastery where the brothers humor and take care of him. Aurelio sees in Columbus's complaint a chance for getting back across the Atlantic. He tells Columbus of the gold and silver and pearls that may be found in the New World, and Columbus instantly recognizes the possibilities. They put together the best clothes that Columbus has and go to see Ferdinand and Isabella of Spain, financing their trip by means of the crushed egg trick that has traditionally been associated with Columbus.

At court, Columbus is able to get the monarchs' attention by having Aurelio speak—something they had never seen before—and then replaying the crushed egg trick for them. Unfortunately the egg spatters all over Ferdinand and Columbus is banished from the court. Aurelio, however, has captured the sympathies of Isabella, who is more temperate and recognizes the importance of a potential source of wealth. Aurelio convinces her to support them, Columbus is brought back, and, despite a series of ridiculous demands by Columbus (he is to be given the title "Admiral of the Ocean Sea"), the monarchs agree to the expedition.

There is still the matter of financing, however, something to which Columbus has not given much thought. Aurelio begins the economics of the trip by pawning two of Isabella's jewels; the rest he finances by flying into the houses of Spain's aristocratic families and looting them for jewels—something that Isabella somehow sees as fitting, as they did not give the jewels to the monarchy during the recent Moorish wars.

When Columbus announces that, as the Admiral of the Ocean Sea, he is too busy and too important to actually go on the voyage, the expedition faces a new difficulty, and Aurelio despairs of ever getting back home. Ferdinand interviews a number of admirals, all of which would rather choose the torture of Ferdinand's dungeons than a trip over the edge of a flat sea. Aurelio, however, comes up with another plan. He chooses the young and dashing captain of the guards, Manuel Nicosa, the intended of Maria Mercedes d'Acosta, handmaid to the queen, to be a false admiral. During the parting ceremonies, he is to bring Columbus down into the captain's quarters to confer about the route; as soon as he is below deck, the ships will set out. All goes without difficulty, except that the ship's crew soon finds that Columbus did not want to go principally because of dreadful seasickness, which afflicts him throughout the voyage. But Manuel does turn out to be a strong admiral, and between Aurelio, Manuel, Maria Mercedes (who has stowed away), and the captain Juan de la Coss, the expedition moves along well, despite an aborted mutiny that Aurelio discovers.

When they land in the New World, Aurelio is overcome with joy, flying to the island and eating the fresh fruit that he has been craving. But once on dry land, Columbus becomes unmanageable, putting on airs,

establishing pompous and empty ceremonies, and taking credit for all
the accomplishments of the expedition. Aurelio is outraged and flies
away, skipping from island to island until he is finally able to reach his
own home.

After three months, however, he begins to wonder what has happened to the expedition and to Columbus. Gathering a bag of jewels
from Indian friends, he flies back to find one of the ships wrecked on a
sandbar and the expedition at a standstill; having found no treasure,
Columbus is unable to decide whether he should push on to continue
the search or return empty-handed to Ferdinand and Isabella. Aurelio
gives the bag of jewels to Manuel and Marie Mercedes "to start house-
keeping on" (107) and then flies off to Columbus to rebuke him for suc-
cumbing to the paralysis of despair. He gives Columbus a bag of gold
nuggets and instructs Columbus to forget about the treasure and
instead bring back the news that he has discovered an entirely new
world: "Tell them you've discovered AMERICA! Take back a lot of
plants; sweet potatoes and tobacco and things like that. Take birds and
animals, take fruits and flowers, take a few Indians. Tell them you've
found the greatest, richest, most fertile land in all the world!" (110).
Columbus is convinced, and soon the expedition is headed back to
Spain, bringing news that will give Columbus yet another title: "Great
Discoverer."

Coming off of the success of *Ben and Me,* Lawson found that the
reviewers were generally kind to *I Discover Columbus,* and yet each
pointed out the narrator's irascibility. The reviewer for *Books* called the
novel a "good-natured burlesque" but noted the "unscrupulous parrot's
frankly low opinion of men." Alice Jordan, writing for *Horn Book,* suggested that "very little dignity is left in any of the notables of 1492
when Aurelio is done with them." The reviewer for the *New York Times
Book Review* spoke of the "fun-poking at the great" but tempered this by
calling the story Aurelio's "acidly candid memoirs." The *New Yorker* was
vague on the narrator, settling for a description based on *Ben and Me:*
"another irreverent and highly imaginative interpretation of history."[3]
Each, then, was drawn to Aurelio as the principal speaker and motivator
of the tale.

Aurelio dominates the narrative from the very beginning. "This is the
story told me by Aurelio, the old, old, parrot of Don Tomas Francisco
Glynn of Santa Margarita" (vii), opens the book, and the illustration
shows Robert Lawson himself sitting in a wicker chair, taking dictation
from a fierce and angry-looking parrot who extends one claw menac-

ingly. The scene recalls the opening of several of Hugh Lofting's Dr. Dolittle books, particularly *Doctor Dolittle's Caravan* (1926), which opens with the parrot Polynesia telling stories to Tommy Stubbins, who is feverishly copying them down. But where Polynesia can be humorously crusty, Aurelio can be dangerous, and there is little humor in his stance: "I know that some will dare to question the accuracy of his story," writes Lawson as narrator of the frame, "but this they would never do if they were, as I was, face-to-face with Aurelio. There is a cold yellow gleam in those eyes, there is a keen curve to that huge beak, painfully like a pair of well-sharpened pruning shears, that somehow discourages any doubting of his word" (viii–ix). Thus the stage is set for a supposedly convincing revision of the Columbus story.

Everything that the reader perceives is mediated by Aurelio's fierce eye, and perhaps it is his unrelenting critical vision that is most wearing. The inside cover illustration shows a happy excited Aurelio, flying above the masts of three ships as they sail over the edge of the world, but he is happy only in that he has so manipulated events that he is heading home. In general, his voice is cynical, sour, and even bitter. The reader would be hard-pressed to see Columbus as anything but a vain and arrogant bumpkin—a picture drawn so sharply that it is difficult to understand why Aurelio feels any pity for him at the adventure's end. Characters are alternately silly, greedy, intemperate, and cowardly as Aurelio judges them, with none of the illustrations challenging these perceptions by suggesting that the parrot's "True History" is in fact a mass of his own perceptions—a technique that Lawson had used in *Ben and Me*.

In *I Discover Columbus* Lawson is not interested in having his readers see other sides of history by changing the reader's perspective; he is instead using that new perspective to undercut historical accounts to produce historical fantasy. In Aurelio, Lawson has crafted a character like Amos the mouse, in that here again is a character who is out to set the record straight and whose self-assuredness is markedly different from his companion's clumsiness and naïveté. "Don't be nervous, Chris," Aurelio counsels Columbus as they are about to appear before Ferdinand and Isabella. "Keep your head and let me do most of the talking—and *all* the thinking" (32). When it seems as if the expedition to the New World has no real admiral to lead it, the parrot pipes in cheerfully that "it's fortunate that we have Aurelio" (83). When mutiny threatens, the parrot is the one who decides how it shall be handled: "No bloodshed if we can avoid it. Leave this to Aurelio" (92). And when the expedition seems to have failed utterly, the parrot is there to remind

FROM *I DISCOVER COLUMBUS* BY ROBERT LAWSON. COPYRIGHT 1941 BY
ROBERT LAWSON; (C) RENEWED. BY PERMISSION OF LITTLE, BROWN
AND COMPANY.

Columbus of who should be doing the thinking: " 'Well Chris, you
haven't done so well without Aurelio, have you?' I asked not very
unkindly" (110). Aurelio's description of his tone seems hard to accept.
This cocksureness will become one of the lovable facets of later narrators
that Lawson will use in this genre, principally because at times it will be
gently undercut. But here, where it is not undercut, the trait is combined with a ferociousness that creates an unlikable narrator.

   Three characters escape Aurelio's cynicism and disdain. One is
Manuel Nicosa, whom the illustrations depict as a sturdy, handsome
cavalryman. A reliable and agreeable soldier, temperate and loyally
eager to serve, he is the single male character whose traits are not exaggerated negatively, so that the reader can even forgive his scornful atti-

tude toward the seasick Columbus as justified: " 'Admiral of the Ocean Sea!' he jeered. 'The great Discoverer—Pooh!' " (111). The other two characters spared Aurelio's derision are Isabella and Maria Mercedes, the novel's only two female characters. Lawson portrays Isabella as the quiet power behind the throne. Ferdinand is intemperate, angers easily, and seems unable to cope with difficulties. When Columbus announces that he will not be the admiral to lead the expedition, Ferdinand searches among his other admirals until he finds that none is willing. His response to the impasse is typical: "A fine lot of Admirals I have! A fine lot of expeditions I have! Glorious Ventures, bah! Council's dismissed! Bah! The whole thing's dismissed! Bah! Bah! Bah!" (66). Isabella, by contrast, thoughtfully begins to take charge of the situation, providing the context for Aurelio to come up with his solution. When the expedition seems to flounder for lack of money, she is the one who develops a new source of funding. Clearly behind the bluster of Ferdinand lies the ready competence of Isabella.

The double-page spread illustrating the procession winding down to the three ships about to depart illustrates the discrepancy between the characters of Ferdinand and Isabella. While Columbus looks on, stupidly smiling, Ferdinand stares straight ahead, intensely aware of his kingly dignity, an angry and severe expression set on his face. Here is not one to be trifled with, despite the fact that the procession ahead of him is filled with floundering altar boys swinging the incense a bit too vigorously. Isabella, on the other hand, looks not down toward the ships but directly out to the reader. She leans her head back like a madonna looking to her child, her eyes loving, her smile demure and regal.

Maria Mercedes is similarly competent and loving; in fact, it is striking that aside from the parrot, the female characters are the only ones who are competent in any way in this novel. Maria Mercedes is the one to suggest her beloved cavalryman for the pseudo-admiral; she is the one to stow away on one of the ships out of love, quickly finding that she is able to bring other strengths to the expedition. In fact, Aurelio credits her with the ultimate success of the voyage, "for she spread a gay kindliness through all the fleet" (88). She is busy from dawn to dusk, chatting with the sailors and ministering to the sick, darning and mending, laughing and singing. The accompanying full-page illustration shows a beatific Maria Mercedes, playing the guitar while sitting on corded rope. Manuel stares at her intently, deeply in love, while the sailors look on with exaggerated expressions of love and longing and sweet homesickness (89). Manuel and Maria Mercedes thus become the ultimate couple, both suited to each other, both handsome, both capable and brave and adaptable, both eminently good.

If at first this novel seems quite different from Lawson's other historical fantasies in that it deals little with the American scene, it is quite clear at the end of the book that although the expedition as originally conceived is a failure, Columbus goes back heartened because something even more wonderful than gold and silver has been found: America. Aurelio tells him to return not to bring back a treasure but to bring back something even more wonderful: the news of an entirely new world. And the evidence of this world is not pearls but the most ordinary kind of things: birds, animals, fruit, sweet potatoes, tobacco. The land is a rich one, Aurelio suggests, not because of useless metal, but because it is so fertile. Here is the celebration of the American scene that would be a strong part of Lawson's later works, for in the conclusion the author shows that the motivations behind the expedition pale in significance to the discovery of "the greatest, richest, most fertile land in all the world" (110). This is suggested further by the book's concluding image, where for the first time the two remaining ships head toward a rising rather than a setting sun (113).

In the end, Lawson's positive comic vision comes out—this despite a crabby narrator and generally unlikable characters. Overwhelming everything is the new land that has been found. And it is important in Lawson's vision to see that America is virtually a paradise, a new Eden. Aurelio's early description of the land and its peoples is a description of paradise, where there is abundant food, the climate is always warm, and there is a close relationship between the animal and human worlds. But it is, he points out, a place very different from contemporary America: "No hunter's gun had ever shattered its peace, no ax had ever laid low one of its great trees. No steam-boat ever disturbed the quiet surface of our slow-moving river nor polluted the fragrant air with the reek of its smoke" (4). Here is Lawson recalling a Neverworld of America and lamenting the intrusions that have defaced it. He will continue to celebrate America's natural wonders and the ingenuity that has led to real progress, but there will always be a tension in the celebration.

All of this is in the background of *I Discover Columbus,* however— hidden by the narrator's harangue. If the book cannot be judged a success, it nevertheless sets up some of the context and technique for the author's two later historical fantasies. Or it may be that Lawson fully intended to do what the reviewer for the *New York Times Book Review* suggested: to spoof the textbooks by combining "a robust slap-stick comedy with slyer and somewhat malicious touches of humor."[4] But to be successful, a spoof must be highly controlled. *I Discover Columbus* is not, as the narrator runs away with the meaning.

Mr. Revere and I

In *Mr. Revere and I* (1953) Lawson created one of his most complex narrators. With Franklin's mouse, Columbus's parrot, and Kidd's cat, Lawson uses fictional animals who, for the most part, are one-dimensional in their characters. They change only moderately in the course of the narratives, coming to an affection for their historical figures, although they are never far from this at the beginning of the novels (with the possible exception of Columbus's Aurelio). Any change on their part is limited to their attitudes toward these figures rather than toward any larger movement.

But this is not the case for Paul Revere's horse, the narrator of *Mr. Revere and I*. Her attitude toward her historical figure is deeply affected by her attitude toward surrounding events. And unlike the other narrators, Sherry is a very real horse, although given a much more romantic life than the horse that Revere rode on that fateful April night. That mare, borrowed by Revere once he had crossed the Charles and reached the Cambridge side, was taken by the British and never returned. Sherry, Lawson's creation, has a much longer life with Revere and his family, stretching to both before and after that April night.

But the larger difference in narrative technique between *Mr. Revere and I* and the other historical fantasies is the major shift in attitude that Sherry undergoes. This shift is suggested by the odd juxtapositions of the frontispiece and the title page. The text for the title page is formally bonded, with a very British mantle design atop it. The mare is named Scheherazade—an appropriate name for a character about to tell stories—and she is cited as "late Pride of his Royal Majesty's 14th Regiment of Foot," suggesting a very British orientation. This, however, is undercut on the title page by an American eagle spread across the bottom of the frame, as if to subvert that British orientation.

But that subversion seems even more complete with the accompanying frontispiece. Here the mare peers out, happily it seems, from a very American pasture: a rustic fence, a pig, a cow, and a rooster complete the scene. Beyond the horse a flagpole rises up from the field. It seems out of place in this illustration, yet the American flag it sports suggests clearly that the horse, late His Majesty's, has come to a new owner-

FROM ROBERT LAWSON, *MR. REVERE AND I* (BOSTON: LITTLE, BROWN, 1953). COPYRIGHT 1953 BY ROBERT LAWSON; (C) RENEWED. BY PERMISSION OF LITTLE, BROWN AND COMPANY.

ship—and most probably a new allegiance. In fact, the major narrative conflict of the book is the movement from the mare's allegiance to the British way of life to an allegiance to the freedom represented by the American way of life. It is a change long in development, often coming in uneasy jolts and starts, and is suggested by the change in the mare's name from the formal Scheherazade to that of the informal Sherry—a pet name given her by Revere's family.

The novel opens in Britain, as Scheherazade is parading before the gouty King George III. His owner is Leftenant Sir Cedric Noel Vivian Barnstable, who, the mare asserts, is "in the highest tradition of British Arms" and "the perfect picture of the ideal Military Man"[5]—although clearly his portrait makes him look ridiculous. In fact, his huge nose, protruding teeth ("not greatly different from my own" [6], observes Scheherazade), and oblique chin suggest the image of a horse. Sir Cedric and his horse are being transported to Boston in order to keep the rowdy colonials in line. The mare is proud to be doing this work for her country and rather contemptuous of the colonials.

The voyage over is ghastly and suggests, in a small but significant way, how the British take care of those under them. The horses are poorly fed and stabled; they are never groomed, the stables never cleaned. They are forced to compete with rats for their food, and they never see the sun. By the time they reach Boston they are in no condition to be ridden. Nevertheless, they are pleased to finally arrive in the city and walk on firm ground, despite the angry and sullen appearance of the colonials, who greet them with nothing but jeers.

The British find themselves most unwelcome in Boston, as do the horses. At first they must camp out in the open on Boston Common, but they are finally housed from the winter weather in a drafty stable, where they begin to recover their strength. Come spring, they begin to run races, and Scheherazade finds herself to be the fastest. This is important to Sir Cedric, for he is a heavy gambler and his losses are high. But when Scheherazade loses an important race when a colonial throws an oyster shell across the bridge of her nose, Sir Cedric is forced to sell her to Stinky Nat, who owns a glue factory. The proud Scheherazade becomes a cart horse, pulling refuse through the streets to the glue factory. Humiliated, she avoids contact with Ajax, one of the other horses she knew in her regiment, and while avoiding him one day she causes an accident.

Sam Adams is on the scene and sees her for the fine horse she is. He takes her in the name of the Boston Committee of Correspondence and brings her to Paul Revere, who needs a mount for his work for the committee. A farrier tends her and brings her to the Reveres, a loving family that instantly adopts her and gives her her new name: Sherry. Treated kindly, she is soon her own self, and she finds that she is happy with this boisterous family, despite the fact that Revere does not really know how to ride and that she is confused and upset by the revolutionary activities that seem to center on the house: upset by the rebellious activity but confused because the activities do indeed seem to be justified. This becomes especially obvious when Sherry sees the back of a British soldier who had been beaten for not saluting Sir Cedric briskly enough; Revere helps him desert, and Sherry, while acknowledging the disloyalty of desertion, truly does understand his motivation.

As Revere learns to ride, he takes Sherry all through the back roads of eastern Massachusetts, developing his spy routes. Sherry finds the colonial troops laughable; they have no discipline. But she does acknowledge that they can shoot—a quality that will come into important play later on.

At this point the crisis begins, and Paul and Sherry begin their series of rides for the committee; they ride to Salem and Marblehead to be sure that the British do not land the tea at those ports. Once back in Boston, Revere takes up guard duty to be sure that the tea is not landed there. During the crisis, Revere and Sherry ride back and forth to keep all members of the committee in contact, and after the Boston Tea Party they ride to New York in order to bring the news to that city. Sherry becomes something of a hero—along with Paul Revere—and with her growing love of the Revere family comes a growing pride in her activities, even though they are against the British.

When the British, in response to the dumping of the tea, close the port of Boston, Sherry and Paul ride time and time again out to the other colonies in order to garner support—which they are able to do. But the closing of the port leads to new awarenesses for Sherry: now she not only has begun to admire the Americans but has also seen a particularly malevolent side to the British. At first she recognizes that the closing will bring hardship to her own beloved family, but then she generalizes to the larger colony: "Of course they had flouted His Majesty's authority, but was this a kingly way to avenge a slight—by starving children and old people? . . . For the first time in my life I began to have doubts as to the divine wisdom of the King and his advisors. The glory of his Armed Forces, its Officers and Gentlemen, began to seem shoddy and tarnished" (91). It is a turning point for her.

Revere continues to work with the committee, rushing back and forth to the Congress of all the Colonies in Philadelphia and meeting General Washington himself, for whom he fashions a new set of teeth. Their rides are mostly wintry and uncomfortable, but neither complains, even when they ride up into New Hampshire to warn the Minutemen that the British are planning to remove powder and supplies from Fort William and Mary. Sherry is proud of her work: "Mr. Revere and I were hailed as heroes for our timely warning" (100).

In Boston supplies become scarce and life is no longer easy for Paul Revere, who is now recognized as a rebel. He is almost caught one day by none other than Sir Cedric and Ajax. As a sergeant grabs her bridle, Sherry comes to an important discovery: "Until that moment, I had not fully realized how glorious it was to be free. Free of the everlasting monotony of barracks life, the deadly round of parade and drill, drill and parade . . . free of the brutal grooms, callous officers, stupid overfed stable-mates—like Ajax!" (102–103). It is a crucial realization—a realization of the value of liberty. Finally, Sherry sees what the position of the colonists has been all along. She breaks free—now independently choosing desertion—and escapes through the narrow streets of Boston. Revere must now live across the river in Charlestown, and little by little he ferries his family across, leaving his eldest son to tend the shop, although little enough business is there with the port closed.

Come April, General Gage plans his raid on Lexington and Concord, and once again Revere and Sherry are in the thick of things. Even before plans are fully developed in Boston, Revere has warned John Hancock and Sam Adams in Lexington. When the signal does finally come from the Old North Church, Sherry and Revere begin the famous midnight ride that alerts the spy network and brings out the Minutemen. It is a harrowing ride for Revere. They escape one ambush by jumping a stone wall and riding into a countryside familiar to them but unfamiliar to the British; in fact, it is Sir Cedric and Ajax who follow and end up splashing into a dark pond. At Lexington they have to roust out Hancock and Adams, then head up to Concord.

Here disaster strikes. They are once again caught, but this time Revere is set on foot and Sherry ridden by a British sergeant. But when the soldiers are confused by a shot in the darkness, Revere escapes, heading back to Lexington. Soon after Sherry throws her horseman and, in the last malignant act by the British against her, she is shot in the shoulder while running away. She makes it back to Lexington where she finds Paul, who is deeply moved and overjoyed to see her again. He tends her wound as best he can, first with bits of cloth and then with his own shirt, and resolves that neither he nor she will ever ride again. He leads her back to Boston by side roads and witnesses the flight of the British troops back to the city. Sherry comes to see that because these colonials can indeed shoot, they do have a chance to win their freedom—especially as she has now witnessed the destruction of the strong discipline of the British forces. (It is no small pleasure to see Sir Cedric dashing away at the head of the panicked retreat.)

Once the pair is back in Charlestown, the farrier who had tended Sherry is fetched—this despite Revere's absolute exhaustion—and he pronounces that Sherry will heal, but she will not be able to run as she had been. Revere's comment is telling: "Sherry has suffered the first wound and shed the first blood in our War of Independence. I think that entitles her to an honorable retirement" (149). This is precisely what she enjoys, particularly after the British are forced to evacuate Boston. And when Sherry thinks back on her life—this at the end of her narrative—she does not think back to her days as the pride of the 14th Regiment. She instead thinks about the hard and cold riding of her dispatch days: "They were hard, rough days, and nights, but never, either then or now, have I once regretted that day when I declared my independence and cast in my lot with the champions of Liberty and Freedom" (152).

It is a stirring affirmation and confirms the image on the novel's frontispiece. But it can only come at the end of the narrative, when Sherry has gone over all the events in order and made sense of them. For at the beginning of the novel, Sherry still has some of Scheherazade in her, supremely proud of her British heritage and her military tradition and unable to criticize or even question what is eminently silly and patently absurd. She is unable to sense, for example, the irony of the ships' names that transport her regiment to Boston: the *Unfathomable,* the *Implacable,* the *Incapable,* the *Impossible,* and the *Implausible.* Sherry herself is transported on the *Glorious,* but it is a terribly old, leaky, and mildewy ship. Although Sherry senses the horror of the passage, she is unable to make the leap of recognition to the difficulties that lie behind the British vision of the colonies.

The result is that once Sherry reaches Boston, she adopts the British attitude toward the colonists. This is most evident in her language, used almost always to describe the collective colonists; it is as if she, like the British, can only see the aggregate and not individuals—one of the reasons for the disastrous blindness of the British. Sherry refers to the colonists as "unruly louts" who do not "comport [themselves] with the valor and dignity of true English Gentlemen and Soldiers of the King" (8). They are "stupid, rustic bumpkins" (13), "lanky rustic[s]" (14), "yokels" (16), "churlish peasants" (17, 19), and "low-class ruffians and ne'er-do-wells who were causing an infinite amount of disorder, in a

sneaky underhand way" (25). This is not an attitude that Sherry can easily abandon. Even after she is starting to feel affection for Revere and his
family, she cannot shake her overall vision of the colonials.

Despite this attitude, however, Lawson plants seeds early in the novel
that will bear fruit in Sherry's understanding of the two different worlds
of which she is a part. Certainly the British world is silly: the parades are
for a gouty and unattending king; the officers on horseback fall asleep
while listening to the prayers of a beefy bishop; the great military tradition is represented by the vain and silly Sir Cedric. But early on Sherry
witnesses a darker side: the terrible neglect of the horses, the whipping so
callously and easily assigned to a sergeant at the wharf (a whipping of
which Sir Cedric seems to gleefully approve), the later whipping given to
the soldier who does not salute Sir Cedric promptly, Sir Cedric's gambling, and the meaningless competition that loses Sherry to the
"yokels"—a loss that Sir Cedric takes with clichéd good humor but
amounts to disaster for the innocent Sherry. But perhaps she should have
expected this, for Sir Cedric's gambling put him deeply into debt—
"which of course, was usual and proper for a young officer and Gentleman of His Majesty's Armed Service, but caused me some concern" (27).

That concern is justified, but at this point in the novel it is a concern
centered on Sherry's individual status; it is not yet applied to the cause
of freedom and liberty. It is the movement that has to occur before she
can transform from Scheherazade to Sherry, and for this movement to
occur she must move away from seeing the colonists as "yokels" and
instead see them for what they are: individuals banding together to
fight for their freedom. And to see this, Sherry must get beyond Ajax's
"wise dictum: 'After all, my dear, like 'im or not, your master is your
master' " (34). "Your master is your master"—this is the unthinking
belief that Scheherazade had always subscribed to, not realizing that its
easy complacency leads to a lack of critical awareness that virtually
destroys the soul. Certainly one sees this in Ajax, who refuses to
acknowledge Sherry once she has left his world, who in fact places her in
the aggregate—"civilians"—so that he need not consider her as an individual. This of course is the same process that the British have used on
the colonists; Scheherazade now has an inkling of what the process does.

After Sherry is forced to flee Boston with the Revere family, she
returns to the question of mastery. She realizes that having escaped, she
has, like the deserting soldier before her, cut off connection to the
crown, and she knows that a horse of her upbringing and traditions
should be shocked. But she is instead strangely exhilarated—paradoxi-

cal feelings that must have characterized many in Boston at the time. She suggests that she has "been born again into a new life in a fresh new world" (106). And with that birth comes a rejection of what she had formerly seen as wise advice: " 'Your master is your master,' Ajax had once stupidly said. All very well that, for a dull-minded King's horse, but not for a free and independent Colonial. Mr. Revere was no master—he was my friend, my loved and respected friend. We were not master and slave, we were partners, partners in a great new and shining adventure" (106). And here she realizes what the dehumanizing process employed by the British has led to: instead of partners in a new and shining adventure, the British and the colonials are inevitably at odds.

For Lawson, the process of Sherry learning about mastery, learning about new kinds of relationships begins with a typical Lawson quality: kindness. More than anything else it is the love and concern showered on the horse by the Revere family that brings her to the cause of freedom. It is not a disgust with the British way of life after she has been sold. It is not her sight of explicit British cruelty. It is not even her work for the revolutionary cause, although that comes to bring her great pleasure. It is her growing love for the family that brings her to the colonial side; it is as if she had to learn to know an individual colonial family before this transformation could occur.

The first illustration of Revere is the book's first illustration of a figure that is not a caricature; it depicts a craftsman seriously engaged in his profession. At first, it is this dedication to craft that impresses the horse, then Revere's attention to healing Sherry. The children all care for the horse, keeping the stall immaculate and bringing her to the freedom of the backyard. Soon Sherry, still caught up in her British traditions, is yet able to conclude that "altogether it was a loving, kindly family and I could not help growing fond of them, even though they were only middle-class tradespeople—and, of course, rebellious Colonials" (48).

Life with the family, however, leads to Sherry's awakening. She compares the care given to her as an army horse to that given to her by a loving family. She sees that the colonials pay their bills to Revere, even if it is with produce, while the British rarely pay. She listens to the free (though covert) talk of politics, and even though she is aghast at the disloyal nature of the talk, she does find the argumentation convincing. She quickly comes to conclude that "I now had the kindliest master ever a horse had, even though he was misguided" (51). The narrative action will bring Sherry even to reject the idea of a kindly master; Revere will become something much more.

Soon Sherry recognizes the real love of the family, and she begins to return it; one cannot love a master, no matter how benevolent. When they are forced to remain in New York over Christmas, both Sherry and Revere are deeply saddened at not being with the family. When they do arrive home, Sherry's stable has been liberally decorated with carrots and apples and Indian corn, and the accompanying picture—again, one of the few that is not a caricature—shows a loving familial embrace for the horse. This love finally transforms Scheherazade to Sherry. When she recognizes the hardship that General Gage's closing of Boston will have on her family, she begins her real rejection of the British tradition.

In *Mr. Revere and I,* Lawson has created his most successful narrator. There is an internal integrity to the character throughout the narrative, as well as a growth that is halting and jerking—as all growth is—but that is consistent with the narrative action. And unlike Franklin's Amos, Captain Kidd's McDermot, and Columbus's Aurelio, this is a character who seems less fantastic in that she is driven by historic events, rather than driving them. This is not Aurelio setting off an expedition to a new world but a character who finds herself caught up in a swirl of events and who must react to them. Her growth is her reaction.

Captain Kidd's Cat

Robert Lawson's final historical fantasy, *Captain Kidd's Cat* (1956), is in many ways his darkest. It lacks the humor of *Ben and Me,* the cynical narrator's manipulation of *I Discover Columbus,* and the growth of the narrator of *Mr. Revere and I.* It also lacks the narrative stance that typifies the other historical fantasies: from the beginning McDermot is a narrator who is really fond of the subject, who in fact sees himself as a part of a team. McDermot the cat could not be more different from Aurelio the parrot; he is to Kidd what Sherry is to Paul Revere late in the novel.

Throughout the text there is a repeated refrain, however: things are going to turn out badly. McDermot has an uncanny ability to sense danger, and he senses it throughout the text. Once he leaves his home at Captain's Rest, he is never settled again until he finds his way back to another Captain's Rest. Meanwhile, he is repeatedly warning Captain Kidd about the wiles of those who make promises to him and that the adventure in which they are both engaged is to be plagued with ill-luck. And if the cat is not enough, Kidd is also warned by his friends that there are bad things in store for him if he continues on his adventure.

Never for a moment does Lawson let the reader believe that all shall be well. His reminders hang over the narrative like gloomy clouds.

In fact, the foreword to the novel is uncommonly open about the coming conclusion, as McDermot reveals his motivations for telling the tale: "Poor Bill! A quiet, respectable New York merchant (that is, as respectable as most), hanged at Execution Dock, wrote about and sung about by ballad hawkers, preached about by parsons, held up to young 'uns as a Horrible Example—and why? I know why and I'll tell it in my own way and in my own time."[6] Although the tone here makes McDermot sound as prickly as Aurelio, in fact the tone is generated by McDermot's perception that Bill Kidd has been duped and bears the blame for the criminal misdoings of "the high and mighty Lords of the Admiralty" (4–5). The result is that the novel stands as an attempt to revive the reputation of William Kidd (ca. 1645–1701). Essentially Lawson is doing the opposite of what he had done in *I Discover Columbus;* instead of debunking, he is reinterpreting in a much more favorable light.

The novel begins at Captain's Rest, a manorial home owned by Captain Tew above Newport, Rhode Island. Tew is a retired pirate, using his wealth to lead him into comfortable old age. McDermot, his cat, anticipates a similar life of easy decline. But Tew receives word that a new governor is coming to the colonies—one who has the backing of the king and is ostensibly determined to rid the seas of pirates. Tew is outraged, for it will mean the destruction of a profitable trade; he resolves to go to sea once more for a last voyage before the governor takes over; with it he will be able to bring home enough money to satisfy his men, who fear that no occupation will be left to them. He leaves McDermot with his friend, Bill Kidd, a merchant (though a former pirate) now living in New York.

McDermot finds it to be an uneasy household; Madame Kidd is a tyrant who completely dominates Kidd. She allows the cat to stay only because he can keep the mice and rats down, thus protecting the household goods. But Captain Kidd finds that life is to be upset for him, just as for McDermot. At a gathering of merchants, Kidd finds that a Mr. Livingston has taken stock in the galley that the king has sent to rid the seas of pirates. This creates an uproar, for the pirates are the very ones who have made—and continue to make—the merchants wealthy. But Mr. Livingston has a plan. Kidd himself will captain the *Adventure* galley.

Kidd refuses; most of the pirates are his close friends and colleagues. But Livingston points out that he needn't actually attack any pirates; he could take the ship and capture any French merchantmen, as England is at war with France. Such captures would be completely legal, and would be supported by the king and the lords of admiralty. Kidd remains unaware that the king and lords are doing this so that they may become wealthy, themselves having taken stock in the *Adventure* as part owners. McDermot, however, is not fooled.

Though unwilling, Kidd is eventually bullied by the merchants and his wife into going to London to meet the king and to see about the commission; once there, he is forced to accept the position as captain. He returns to New York and prepares to set out with McDermot, resolving to make two captures of French merchantmen—enough to satisfy the greed of the owners—and to be sure to avoid any pirates.

In the latter he is very successful. He sends messages ahead to warn the pirates of the arrival of his ship, and he flies a distinguishing pennant to be sure that he will not face his former colleagues. They avoid him completely—his avowed objective. But while this element of the voyage is a success, the other is a crashing failure. He is not able to sight any merchantmen that are possible targets, and after a fruitless year of wandering the oceans, his men become at first frustrated and then quite angry. They have some small adventures. They escape by using their sweeps from a British fleet about to impress some of Kidd's sailors. They have a small brush with an East Indiaman, protected by the British crown, and eventually blow the figurehead off the merchant ship. A third of the crew is lost to cholera when they land on one island, and soon after they are chased away from a group of Armenian merchantmen when they are believed to be pirates. Nothing seems to change the voyage's luck, as McDermot continues to point out.

But then the ship does turn piratical; when they meet another Armenian merchantman—not a suitable target, as it is not French—some of Kidd's men take the gig and ransack the ship, getting almost nothing. They are branded as pirates for this act, however, and Kidd has to avoid several Portuguese ships that attack him. Bill is angry, but not nearly as angry as the day he sees one of his men attack McDermot. Kidd heaves a wooden bucket at the offender, who dies the next day of cholera.

Soon afterwards, Kidd does capture a rich merchantman, big enough and wealthy enough for him to return home. But by now his crew is mutinous, and when they have to ground the *Adventure* because of its numerous leaks, many of them jump ship for that of one of Kidd's former colleagues, Captain Culliford. Culliford eventually protects Kidd from his own crew, and Kidd sails away in the merchantman, having

kept all of the ship's stores except for the gold and silver that he distributed evenly to his men. When he reaches the Caribbean, however, he
hears news that he is now considered a pirate. Kidd cannot understand
this; he is unable to see as McDermot has all along that the men who
established his mission were scoundrels. In fact, word has got out that
the king and the lords had hired Kidd to, in effect, attack merchantmen
instead of pirates for their own gain; the high and mighty, as McDermot
calls them, are embarrassed by the scandal, and instead they argue that
Kidd has simply turned pirate. They, too, call for his capture. When Bill
returns to New York, he cannot believe that his fellow merchants and
English nobles would be so dishonorable. He is arrested, all evidence of
his innocence is destroyed, and he is sent to Newgate Prison in London,
there to await trial.

He waits two full years, all the time writing letters to those he supposed were his friends, all fruitless. After the trial he entrusts McDermot
to the jailor Kistdale, who promises to find him a home back in the
colonies. But he, too, is not to be trusted; he puts McDermot on display,
along with the other artifacts of the "wicked" Kidd's career, and charges
admission to the gullible, sticking McDermot with a wire to make him
ferocious. Right after Kidd is executed, Kistdale takes McDermot to
New York; leaving London, McDermot avoids looking at the bridge
where Kidd's body is hanging.

In New York, Kistdale takes McDermot to an inn curiously called
the Captain's Rest. It is owned by Captain Tew's former slaves; they
were released when he died during his last voyage. The inn's owners
release McDermot from his cage, and after the cat claws Kistdale's ears,
he settles down to a new life and into a comfortable old age at Captain's
Rest. And yet, it is not completely comfortable; there is the disturbing
knowledge of the body hanging by the bridge, and the dreadful duplic-
ity of humanity. The concluding line, given as a toast at the inn, suggests the great tragedy of the novel: "To our friend Will Kidd, Merchant, Captain and Gentleman. He trusted too many too far" (152);
beneath this line Lawson pictures McDermot, curled up and asleep. He
is the one character throughout the novel who is perceptive and recognizes the dangers that Kidd's friends and the officials of the town pose.
But Kidd seems forced by circumstances into a position from which
there is no escape. He ends dreadfully, through no fault of his own.

Kidd is a much more complicated figure than any of the other central
characters in Lawson's historical fantasies. When Lawson first introduces
him, he seems to stand in a stark contrast to the rugged Captain Tew.

True, he has been a pirate like Tew, but now he is settled into the life of a merchant, running a small though prosperous shop. Tew seems to dominate him physically in Lawson's first illustration of the two together (13); he stands over Kidd, dressed as the gallant and robust pirate, a man of action and resolve approaching a merchant. Even McDermot is unimpressed with Kidd's first appearance, suggesting that Kidd is as different from a pirate captain as a canoe is different from a ship of the line: "A meek-and-mild-seeming little man, with his neat-arranged hair and sober dark clothes, looking more like a country parson or a countinghouse clerk than a seafaring man. In fact, seeing a quill stuck behind his ear, I thought he was a clerk, till him and Captain Tew began whoppin' and poundin' each other on the back the way sailors always do. He was sailorlike too, the quick way he skipped over to a cupboard and set out a bottle of Madeira and two glasses" (14). Kidd seems to have two different natures here, not fully integrated—although it is to be remembered that this is all from McDermot's perspective. On the one hand he is the counting-house clerk keeping minute accounts of the goods held in his basement. Certainly his face and demeanor as depicted in the early illustrations suggests that side of his personality. And yet there is the sense that he, too, is one among the brotherhood of pirates. He has the sea-goers rolling gait, the quick and assumed manners of hospitality, the decisive air, and the boisterous manners brought on by seeing an old pirate friend.

Throughout the early parts of the novel, however, these two sides are not at all integrated. In the presence of his wife, he becomes one of Lawson's typically exaggerated characters. When she first sees McDermot, she explodes:

"What is that?"

"A cat, my dear, just a cat," Kidd says, all of a sweat, "a very well-trained, useful cat . . ."

"You may keep him—for a while," she says finally. "But mind you, he is not to set foot above stairs . . ."

"Yes, my dear, thank you, my dear," Kidd says. (19–20)

This is Lawson's milquetoast husband, exaggerated and simplified to a stock character. This side of Kidd's personality seems to be confirmed when he is manipulated by the merchants of New York into accepting the captaincy of a ship for that he has no interest (it is actually the fear of his wife which makes him finally accept). The illustration for this moment pictures Kidd with his hands held up in denial and refusal, but the officials around him hold up their hands as well—in toast to the success of his voyage. Livingston, who has just manipulated him into this position, sits with a satisfied, self-assured smirk. But what is most telling is the group in the foreground, where one merchant whispers to another, the malicious and sneering laughter on his face suggesting that he knows the position that is being set up, knows that Kidd would be what was known in later times as "the fall guy" (25).

McDermot's role in this illustration establishes his attitude toward both the merchants and toward Kidd. He stares at Livingston, back arched, hair bristling, ears back, hissing. Clearly he has established an alliance with Kidd—a significant moment in the novel, because McDermot has been characterized as a cat with a peculiarly accurate sense of judgment. He is able to perceive the nature of one's character.

At first it is difficult to accept this sense of perception, for McDermot so quickly is willing to leave Tew and accept Kidd, even trying hard to satisfy him by gifts of dead rodents. McDermot is able to see deeper than do the merchants, however. They see Kidd as gullible, easily maneuvered, and innocent—and he is that. But McDermot sees him as a real sea captain beneath his clerk's persona. Once they have put to sea, Kidd is transformed. The first illustration depicting him as captain shows him standing straight, a telescope tucked under his arm, his face set and stern. He is clearly in command. McDermot notices this as well: "It was good, too, to see how fast Bill shed his Pearl Street meekness and became a man again. Every league we put between us and Madame made him more of a captain. Not that he was ever any roaring bully, like Avery of Ireland, but he knew his business and in his quiet way he had an educated tongue that could rip the hide of the toughest old shellback and set him skipping" (40). McDermot's story is not just of the voyage but of the integration of these two sides of Kidd's character: the one gentle and unassuming, the other stern and piratical. And if that integration leads to tragedy, it also leads to wholeness.

Throughout the voyage Kidd remains concerned with finding a Turkish carpet for his wife, of a certain size and a certain color. He searches for it constantly, and at one point he risks his ship in trying to trade with a merchantman. Here is the side of him that continues to show his timidity. When he returns to New York with the carpet, his wife takes it from him and leaves him to his fate; her concern has all along been the rug and her social status. The illustration depicting the exchange characterizes Kidd once again as the milquetoast husband (117).

FROM ROBERT LAWSON, *CAPTAIN KIDD'S CAT* (BOSTON: LITTLE, BROWN, 1956). REPRINTED BY PERMISSION OF MARTIN BRIGHT AND THE NINA I. BOWMAN ESTATE.

And yet most of the narrative focuses on Kidd's successes as a captain—not in terms of taking prizes but in terms of acting out his piratical role. When his ship is threatened by three British wars that intend to impress many of his men, he manages a clever escape in the darkness. When his men come down with cholera, he is the one who tends them all. When a Portuguese man-of-war comes upon them and attacks,

Kidd, though vastly outgunned, comes off the better: "Bill was the fightingest mad captain ever I see. I began to take in now why he'd been a holy terror to the Frenchies when he was a privateersman" (69). His personal courage is unquestioned. When Moore the gunner attacks McDermot, Kidd lays him low with a bucket. When the crew mutinies for lack of prizes and the ship is grounded, Kidd shows no fear. With only McDermot and four companions, he is ready to hold out against the mutineers.

The tremendous irony of the book is that the very things that show Kidd's courage and resoluteness are the same things that are later re-interpreted by those whom he had trusted. In their reinterpretation, Kidd becomes a bloodthirsty pirate, an example to children of what not to be, the subject of sermon illustrations, reviled and attacked by those who had asked him to do the very thing he has done. It is said that Kidd attacked other ships and destroyed them, killing their crews, that he murdered Moore in cold blood, that he murdered a tribe that lived peacefully on an island, that he had hidden vast amounts of treasure stolen during his voyage. His sailor's instinct fails him when he approaches land, and he is unable to believe that charges will be pressed against him. Unfortunately he is quite wrong.

McDermot ascribes Kidd's fate to the bad luck of the venture. The cat repeatedly refers to the ill-fortune that seems to follow them. During the fight with the man-of-war, the cat observes that they could have sunk the larger ship: "In a wind she'd have been helpless then and there, but with our usual luck there wasn't a breath; it was almost a dead calm" (70). When the cholera is cured, McDermot is still not cheered: "The strange thing was, though, that spite of this turn for the better, that feeling of gloom that had settled in my bones didn't light at all. Fact is, it got worse" (63). This kind of line recurs throughout the text, as though Lawson never wishes his reader to forget that the cat ascribes all of this to chance. And certainly there is something to this; Kidd and his crew simply never meet up with a prize until the crew is so mutinous as to be almost uncontrollable, and in the interval the wind of politics has led to a situation where the captain must be sacrificed in order to preserve the "honor" of the nobility. Perhaps this is all bad luck.

Like any tragedy, however, this one has its seeds in character. Kidd is weakest on land, easily manipulated, and that is where all the machinations behind the voyage are made. His prowess on the sea cannot compete with backroom politics, especially when the king is involved. On the sea he must trust himself, and that he can do. On land he must trust princes, and that, he finds, leads to disaster. McDermot's assertion in the foreword suggests that loyalty is a large theme in this story. In fact, the novel might be read as a study in loyalty, as Kidd holds true to his work only to find that those he considered his friends do not. As he sails into New York, he looks across at the horizon and realizes with yearning that his world is becoming smaller and smaller as he is abandoned: " 'Well, there it is, old cat,' he says, 'the goal of all our dreams—warm spring evening, cherry trees, fat burghers, shaded arbors and all the homecoming heart could desire. Unfortunately, however, we are off shore, looking on' " (115).

Soon even that situation will be reversed, as he and McDermot become spectacles rather than spectators. They become the stuff of myth, crowds scrambling to get a look at them as they are brought from one prison to another. And myths have no real personhood any longer; no one responds to Kidd's letters—not his friends, wife, or colleagues. In the end, he realizes that all that is left to him is to perform as a spectacle, and he sells McDermot's ruby earring to buy a fine suit of clothes for what the jailor calls "the occasion." And McDermot himself becomes a spectacle, one of the horrible artifacts from Kidd's piracy. And that is why, at the end of the novel, McDermot refuses to play the role of spectator and look at Kidd's body.

It is in prison that Kidd becomes the fully integrated person. He comes to realize and accept—he cannot do otherwise—that the world that he had once been so much a part of, the wealthy New York aristocracy, is in fact a corrupt mass. They have tried to reinvent Kidd to save themselves, and when Kidd recounts that reinvention, McDermot replies with his usual perception:

> "So you see, Mac, old cat, I am a most reprehensible, gory-handed villain, traitor, freebooter and murderer. Not at all a fit companion for an honest pirate cat such as you. I am surprised that you can put up with me."
> There wasn't much I could do but knead his leg and purr a bit, but I didn't feel much like purring. (135)

Kidd's last act is one of kindness; he sells the ruby to Kistdale, the jailor, anticipating that he will remove it cleanly and painlessly so that McDermot will not be killed for it by someone else, and he arranges to have McDermot taken back to New York: "The cherry trees should be in bloom along the Bouwerie now. Enjoy them to the fullest, Mac—for both of us" (139). This is the last word that we hear from Kidd, and it is appropriate that it is a word of friendship.

In the end, McDermot rejects the lesson that Kidd apparently learns: that one should not trust. Just as Kidd remains faithful to him, the cat remains faithful to Kidd's memory, as do the others at the Captain's Rest. If the world is corrupt, still, one lives as though it were not. And though such a choice may lead to tragedy (as it does in Kidd's case), it may also lead one to a small group of kindred souls whose faithfulness belies the essential nature of the world. This faithfulness is what saves the book from being merely a tragedy, and perhaps this is what allows the book to be read today as children's literature. If it has not achieved the fame of *Ben and Me,* perhaps it is not just because *Captain Kidd's Cat* was not made into a film. Perhaps it is because the meanings of *Captain Kidd's Cat* are harder to perceive. Joy hidden beneath tragedy usually is.

Chapter Four
The Rabbit Hill Books

In the 1940s Robert Lawson composed a series of novels set around his own country home in Connecticut; they were not universally successful. Where they did succeed, they forged a strong union between country setting, the animal inhabitants of that setting, the sympathetic perceptions of the inhabitants of the Big House up the hill, and the wry observations of the narrator. In one way the world of Rabbit Hill is the major figure of these works—a world seen bucolically in *Rabbit Hill* (1944) and *The Tough Winter* (1954) and as a site for fantasy in *Robbut: A Tale of Tails* (1948) and *Edward, Hoppy and Joe* (1952). In each case, Rabbit Hill is more than setting; it is a world set apart, with its own rules that determine the human and animal stories that will play themselves out.

It is almost indisputable that *Rabbit Hill* and *The Tough Winter* are Lawson's most successful works. Both are marked by a narrative tightness, progression, and pleasing inevitably that are not qualities of his more diffuse and whimsical fantasies. Here the interplay between fantasy and realism, the single setting, the clearly differentiated characters, and the simplicity of the plot line all merge to form fantasies that, to use the words of most contemporary reviewers, amuse and delight. The bucolic vision that Lawson creates plays on several different levels: nostalgia, an empathetic relationship with the natural world, and a deeply felt spiritual sense of fecundity and fullness. The natural world invoked in these novels is idyllic, and the human presence in this world is complementary, not adversarial.

This bucolic vision means that the interplay in the novels between fantasy and reality—the advent of New Folks in a house and the various perspectives on those Folks from the points of view of the small animals—is skewed strongly to the fantasy side of things, in that it is a world with no real threats. Certainly the Folks hold an enormous love and gentle respect for the surrounding wildlife, but the sense of community and wholeness that marks the life of the small animals in these novels is gentle as well, so that there seems to be no competition in the animal world, no hunting (except for the hunting of hens and chickens, which are domesticated and therefore seem not to count), no real danger except that of hunger.

It is as though *Rabbit Hill* were on one end of a spectrum and Richard Adams's *Watership Down* on another. The first marks a group of animals in cooperation and peace; the second marks a group of animals threatened by humanity and threatened by each other, never mind other animal predators. Thus the claim of the *Saturday Review of Literature*'s critic is misleading: "We have seldom had for children so convincing a picture of rabbits—real, wild New England rabbits."[1] In fact, neither *Rabbit Hill* nor *The Tough Winter* offers a convincing picture of the real life of wild New England rabbits. But this is not what Lawson, with gentle fantasy in mind, set out to do.

Rabbit Hill

Illustrated in the midst of a world war, the endpages of *Rabbit Hill* must have seemed astonishingly peaceful to contemporary readers; the sense of peace must itself have generated a sense of fantasy. Rabbit Hill is pictured at the bottom of an easily sloping valley; the stone house with its additions is surrounded by formal gardens, a broad expanse of lawn, and grape arbors. Behind it stretches a vast garden; in front is the North Field and pine woods. By the garden is a fountain surrounded by trees and graced by the statue of Saint Francis, who holds out his hands in blessing. The driveway meanders out to a small road that heads "up Danbury way,"[2] but there is no traffic to disturb the serenity. All is surrounded by one of the old stone walls of New England, lending not only a sense of enclosure but of security as well. Tim McGrath's fenced-in garden on the other side of the road is clearly meant to keep animals out; the stone wall around Rabbit Hill is meant to protect.

What is striking about the illustration, however—and this has implications for the treatment of the text—is how grossly oversized the animals are. The homes of each are drawn in, but they themselves are out of all perspective, much larger than they should be. The reason for this lies with another sense of perspective—the point of view of the animals. To them, the scenery is irrelevant; what is important is how the world of Rabbit Hill provides for their needs, as well as the locale of their home. The endpages are thus a subtle way of shifting the reader's focus to the perspective of the animal inhabitants of Rabbit Hill, and this shift is crucial if the novel is to work as a successful fantasy; the reader must see through the eyes of the animals if he or she is to understand the tension they feel over the coming of the New Folks.

The coming of the New Folks is what provides the narrative impetus for *Rabbit Hill*. The novel begins with the announcement of their coming: "All the Hill was boiling with excitement. On every side there rose a continual chattering and squeaking, whispering and whistling, as the animals discussed the great news. Through it could be heard again and again the words, 'New Folks coming' " (11–12). As the animals gather to discuss the possibility, more and more evidence appears to suggest that they are right. The lawn is cut, the roof is mended, the North Field prepared for planting, the stone wall repaired, the driveway looked to. The question for the animals is a very real one: What kind of Folks will these people be? Will they be the kind with dogs and cats that hunt? with fences around their gardens? with traps and poisons? Will they even be planting Folks at all? The early evidence, however, seems to suggest that all will be well. The back garden is doubled in size, and no fence appears around it. On moving day there is no evidence of traps or poison, and the only domestic animal they bring is a mellow old cat. The garbage that they produce is, from the perspective of the porcupine, just fine.

The first meeting with the New Folks confirms the tenor of this evidence. When the Folks drive in, Father Rabbit rushes past them to see their reaction; they brake quickly and later return with a sign that they post at the head of their driveway: "Please Drive Carefully On Account Of Small Animals" (78). They refuse to allow their gardener to set traps or poison for the mole, even if it means that the grass must be periodically rolled. When Willie Fieldmouse falls through the top of the rain barrel, he is rescued, surrounded by cotton, and fed milk with wine— "He wished he had some more" (91). When Georgie is run over by a speeding car, the New Folks run down to the road, watched by the animals: "They heard the Man say, 'Here, hold the flashlight,' saw him whip off his coat and spread it on the roadway, heard him say 'There now, there now,' as, kneeling, he gently wrapped something in it. They saw him tramp up the driveway carrying the bundle carefully. They saw the Lady's face, white and drawn in the moonlight, and they heard her saying things no Lady should ever say" (102). Georgie's restoration to the animal community is in fact the climax of the novel, representing the kind of relationship established between the New Folks and the animals.

Part of that climax is captured in the final large illustration. The New
Folks have put out a statue of Saint Francis; on it are engraved the
words "There is enough for all." On Midsummer's Eve, the very night
the animals have decreed to be the time when they will divide the produce of the garden among themselves, the New Folks have spread an
array of vegetables at the saint's feet—all for the animals: "There was a
steady sound of chewing and munching and champing. The Folks"—no
longer identified as New Folks—"sat silent, the glow of the Man's pipe
rising and falling with slow regularity" (124). The stately and noble
reaction to this generosity comes from the Red Buck: " 'We have eaten
their food,' his voice rang out impressively. 'We have tasted their salt, we
have drunk their water, and all are good.' He tossed his proud head in
the direction of the garden. 'From now on this is forbidden ground' "
(125–26). In fact, however, he has no need to forbid it, for every night
the area around the saint is filled with produce, so that the garden
remains untouched—a fact that the gardener, Tim McGrath, is unable
to account for. The novel concludes, then, with plentitude, peaceful and
loving relationships, and real joy—both on the part of the New Folks
and on the part of the animals: "All summer, Mother and the other
womenfolk preserved, packed and put away winter stores. Once again
there were parties and merrymaking, laughter and dancing. Good days
had come back to the Hill" (128). This conclusion is illustrated with a
reposed Little Georgie, happily and contentedly asleep by Willie Fieldmouse.

Reviewers focused especially on the world that Lawson had created,
rather than the narrative itself. Anne Eaton, writing for the *New York
Times Book Review,* claimed that "in the case of children particularly, the
broadening of the horizon, the inner spaciousness which the imaginative
book provides, has an importance that cannot be measured. Robert
Lawson, because he loves the Connecticut countryside and the little animals of field and wood and looks at them with the eye of an artist, a
poet and a child, has created for the boy and girl, indeed the sensitive
reader of any age, a whole, fresh, lively, amusing world." The *Saturday
Review of Literature*'s critic described the illustrations as "so vividly pic-
tur[ing] the Connecticut hills that a native of New England exiled to
some far-off outpost would look at them with a lump in his throat. . . .
Rabbit Hill combines a humorous and dramatic story with a background
so authentic and characterization so true."[3] Similarly taken by the landscape, the *Horn Book* reviewer was, however, more able to sense the large
point of that background: "The Connecticut landscape, home of rabbits,

woodchucks, skunks, foxes, field mice and moles, makes an irresistible call in the entrancing pictures. Best of all is the ending of the beautiful book that assures the Little Animals, 'There is enough for all.' "[4] Here in fact is the larger point that informs *Rabbit Hill:* the peaceful and serene affirmation that "There is enough for all."

It is an affirmation that calls for action, however. At the beginning of *Rabbit Hill* and through the action of its sequel, *The Tough Winter,* there is in fact not enough for all. The house on the hill has been deserted, and for some time it has not been inhabited by planting folks. When Mother Rabbit hears the news that New Folks might be coming, she is in the midst of preparing a thin soup: "Well, it's high time there were new Folks in the Big House, high time, and I do hope they're planting Folks, not shiftless like the last ones. Three years now since there's been a good garden on this place. Never enough to put anything up for the winters and last winter the worst in years. I don't know how we ever got through it and I don't know how we'll ever make out if they're not planting Folks, I just don't know, with food getting scarcer all the time and no place to get a vegetable except the Fat-Man's-at-the-Cross-road, and him with his dogs and all, and crossing the Black Road twice a day to get there. I just don't know, I just don't know" (12). The run-on sentence gives a breathless quality to her worry; it has been some time since there was enough. Once the garden is planted, the animals again must face the issue; they must decide not to take the plants too soon and not to take from each other. On Midsummer's Eve, everything in the garden will be divided between them. (There is no understanding yet that much of the garden has been planted specifically for them.) Division ensures that there will be enough for all. But the end of the novel suggests that it is stewardly benevolence that will lead to enough for all, as the New Folks themselves provide for the animals' present and future needs.

The affirmation of plentitude becomes wider than a celebration of mere food, however; the provision of food for the animals becomes a metaphor for a way of living that allows space for all, that suggests the real possibility of lives lived in proximity and peace. This is something that the animals have been practicing all along, but they have not experienced it with the inhabitants of the house on Rabbit Hill. If they have a hope that the New Folks will be planting Folks, they also have a terrible fear: that they may be Folks with traps, poisons, and dogs and cats. In fact, the New Folks craft a home where the animals are not only threatened but actively protected. There is enough for all in terms of space, as well as food.

While this concern is optimistic and affirming, perhaps even ideal-
ized, it is not necessarily the source of the amusement and delight that
reviewers identified. The reviewer for the *New Yorker* argued that *Rabbit
Hill* was an Americanized *Wind in the Willows*.[5] If the reviewer meant by
this to equate the two books' complexity of theme and writing style, he
is probably wrong. If he meant to equate the development and differen-
tiation of character between the two books, he has exaggerated. But if
he meant to equate the fusion of character, landscape, and theme, then
there is a strong case. Like Kenneth Grahame, Lawson created characters who are intimately tied to the landscape—in fact, they could not be
imagined outside of that landscape—and it is in this very tie that much
of the novel's meaning lies.

Here again the illustrations for the endpages come into play. *Rabbit
Hill* is a bound world, like Robert McCloskey's islands, where characters
move and have their being in a relatively secure setting. They may go
out from that setting—in McCloskey to Buck's Harbor, in *Rabbit Hill*
up Danbury way—but they inevitably return to the security of their
bound world. And each has his place in that world; just as the animals
would divide up the produce of the garden, so they have divided up the
land on the Hill, so that each is identified with a specific area—the Red
Buck with the North Field, the skunk with the "Free Garbidge," the
mole by the rolling lawn. There is a sense of appropriateness in all of
this, as though the setting and the characters are one, and that union is
right and good.

It is so right and so good that even natural enmities have dissipated.
When Father Rabbit meets the Gray Fox, their connection is surprising
but real: " 'I must thank you,' the Fox went on, 'for taking those dogs
off my trail yesterday morning. I wasn't in very good condition to deal
with them. You see, I had been away up Weston way to bring home a
hen—pickings are pretty scarce hereabouts these days. Eight miles it is,
there and back, and she was a tough old girl. She was sitting pretty
heavy and I was tuckered out when those dogs jumped me. You handled
them very skillfully, very, and I am obliged to you' " (18). Hens, of
course, as domesticated animals, are outside of the boundaries of *Rabbit
Hill*'s peace and suitable division.

What is most remarkable from the animals' point of view is that the
New Folks fit into this scheme as well. The point of view—always that
of the animals—recalls McCloskey's duck's-eye-view in *Make Way for
Ducklings:* the reader is constantly having the action of the narrative

interpreted through the eyes of the animals. In fact, because this is the focus, it is perhaps not surprising that the New Folks do not actually arrive on the scene until halfway through the novel, for Lawson is interested in the lives of the animals, particularly their hopes and fears about this new situation. Lawson's encouragement here, then, is to have the reader participate imaginatively in the lives of his rabbits.

When Father sends Little Georgie up Danbury way, he takes the time to instruct him: "Now attend carefully. Size up your dog; don't waste speed on a plodder, you may need it later. If he's a rusher, check, double and freeze. Your freeze, by the way, is still rather bad. You have a tendency to flick your left ear, you must watch that. The High Ridge is very open country so keep in the shadow of the stone walls and mark the earth piles. Porkey has lots of relatives along there and if you are pressed hard, any of them will gladly take you in. Just tell them who you are, and don't forget to thank them. After a chase, hide up and take at least ten minutes rest. And if you have to really run, tighten that knapsack strap, lace back your ears, put your stomach to the ground and RUN!" (37–38). Father sounds a bit like Polonius here, but what Lawson has tried to evoke is the animals' perspective. The reader is seeing rabbit strategies from the inside. This perspective has been so strongly established by the novel's conclusion that the reader is in the same position as the animals.

The New Folks always remain somewhat distant; nothing is seen from their perspective, although it is clear that their concerns mirror those of the animals. When the mason starts to rebuild the stone wall, the New Folks ask him to leave one tumbled-down section because "there's a woodchuck living under there and we really shouldn't disturb him" (28). When Tim wants to fence the garden, the New Folks again respond in a way that mirrors the animals' point of view, as Tim tells Louie:

> I was telling them they ought to build a fence around that garden. . . .
>
> And what do you suppose she sez to that? . . . "We like 'em," she sez. "They're so beautiful," she sez. Beautiful, mind you. "And they must be hungry too," sez she.
>
> "You're right, ma'am," I sez. "They're hungry all right, as you'll learn to your sorrow," I sez, "when them vegetables come up."
>
> And then he chips in, the man. "Oh, I guess we'll get along all right with 'em," sez he. "I think there'll be enough for all of us"—us mind you, "that's why we planned the garden so big," he sez. (83–84)

The perspective of Louie and Tim is the conventional human perspective; that of the New Folks is close to that of the animals; they recognize the need for a big garden—enough for all—and for tumbled-down walls for woodchucks.

Lawson is doing here what he has done in his historical fantasies: merging the very real with the fantastic. This comes out dramatically in Father's speech: Little Georgie runs and freezes, but he also carries a knapsack; he hides in burrows, but he is also obliged to thank the occupants. It is a union that is also maintained in the illustrations. The first illustration of Gray Squirrel is quite realistic, but as he scratches behind his ear he looks puzzled, for he has forgotten where his store of nuts is buried. The first illustration of Mother, Father, and Little Georgie is much more humanized; Mother holds a wooden spoon, her paw up to her face in dismay; Little George is asleep on a bunk, under a blanket (27).

This union of the fantastic with the real is also a strategy for characterization. Little Georgie is the impetuous, energetic child, famed for his running and able to leap wide streams in a single bound. Father is the southern gentleman who wanders graciously among his neighbors, recalling the splendid days of his southern life. His neighbors are not interested, however: " 'I always enjoy a run to hounds. Brought up on it, you know. Why, down in the Bluegrass Country—' 'Yes, I know,' said the Fox hastily" (19). Mother is the worrier, a quality which becomes paralyzing when Georgie is hurt, as she takes to her bed, making no plans for canning or preserving. And Uncle Analdas is the curmudgeon; for him, all the good times are in the past and the future is likely to be filled with traps and poison.

The humanization of the animals is so strong that it seems to spill over into the human world of the narrative. When Little Georgie is excited by his leap over Deadman's Brook, he comes up with a song to sing about the New Folks: "New Folks coming, Oh my!" (45). He sings it on his way home from Danbury way, and by the time he reaches home all the animals are singing it: "All over the Hill the voices of the Little Animals were rising in a chorus, and they were singing his song—the Song of Little Georgie!" (57). Porkey takes it up, then Willie Fieldmouse, then Uncle Analdas, and then suddenly even the carpenters are whistling the tune, and Tim McGrath the gardener, and his wife, and Louie the mason, and even Mr. Daley down at the corner store, who makes no other appearance in this novel but to suggest the merger of the human and animal worlds.

Lawson has crafted a novel where the characterization, the actors, and the landscape all point to the union of the human and animal, a union made possible by the recognition that there is enough for all. "Real sensible, knowledgeable Folks they seem to be" (79), the animals conclude. Tim and Louie conclude that the Folks are rather queer, the fault of reading too many books. And it is hard to say what Lawson himself feels about these New Folks and their ways. The temptation in this novel is to equate the New Folks with the Lawsons. Marie Lawson's biographical article that follows the Newbery acceptance speech in *Horn Book* is entitled "Master of *Rabbit Hill,* Robert Lawson," and the accompanying photographs seem to take pains to show the union of the real-life estate with the grounds of the fictional world Lawson has created for the novel. But the Newbery speech itself does not make this union; it seems at times to consciously reject it. "When this book was first going on," Lawson wrote, "I told May [Massee] very firmly that no matter what happened, I was not going to wear the flowering tie and a buckskin shirt and go around doing bird-calls and posing as a nature lover, and I'm not going to start now." Much of the speech is in fact a repudiation of the New Folks' attitudes, as he discusses the killing and trapping of moles, their rejection of a vegetable garden, their accommodations to the wildlife that are truly one-sided: "We do have all the animals mentioned and we do get along quite amiably, but it is a thing that takes considerable compromising and adjustment"; the New Folks would go further than this in their active creation of a secure and bountiful place where "There is enough for all."

Robbut: A Tale of Tails

Four years after *Rabbit Hill,* Lawson returned to the animals around his home as a source for story. *Robbut: A Tale of Tails* came out in 1948 and earned Lawson some of his first less-than-favorable reviews. They were deserved. *Kirkus Review* called it "second string Lawson," and the *New York Times Book Review* praised the beauty and design of the book but complained about the lack of characters in a book that "becomes slightly monotonous." The complaints were not universal, however. The *Saturday Review of Literature* referred to it as "this delightful and mirth-provoking book" and suggested that it was "as lovable and appealing as *Rabbit Hill.*"[6] "Lovable" and "appealing" are extraordinarily subjective terms, and perhaps this reviewer truly believed that assessment. But 50 years of distance may provide some balance, for this is not one of Lawson's more successful works.

The story is didactic and marred by its obviousness and predictability. Robbut is unhappy with his small tail and yearns for something more useful and beautiful. The illustration for the endpages show a mournful Robbut looking up into the clouds and imagining all sorts of tails that are ever so much more appealing: a striped cat's tail for beauty, a fox's tail for warmth, a cow's tail for usefulness, a skunk's tail for authority, a squirrel's tail for its bushiness. Robbut has the opportunity to fulfill his wishes when he rescues a strange Little Man from a trap set out by the owners of the Big House up the hill. The man brings Robbut to his house within a tree, and there offers him a reward: he may choose another tail if he wishes.

So begins the triptych of Robbut's three adventures. He chooses a large, striped cat's tail for this first try: "Robbut viewed himself and his new tail from every possible angle. The more he looked the greater were his pride and joy. He strode past with his tail straight up, quivering with pleasure, just the tip of it swaying slightly. He lashed it as though he were angry until it pounded his ribs and raised clouds of dust from the rug. He lay down and waved it in slow, stately, pleased circles. He swung it around until it tickled his chin and he could stroke it with his forepaws. He did everything with it a Cat could do and some things only a Rabbit would think of."[7] The pride, the pleasure, the self-satisfied stance will all be questioned almost immediately, however: when he leaves the Little Man's house, he slams the door on his new tail. It is only the first of his difficulties. When he goes into the fields, the grasshoppers jeer at him for trying to be something he is not. The birds attack him because they think he is a cat on the prowl, and the other animals—his friends—flee as well. The Lady of the Big House sends her son to throw rocks and scare off the strange cat, and the tail is muddied and full of briars that tear out its hair. Robbut crawls back to the house of the strange Little Man but must spend the cold, wet night waiting for him.

Robbut has not learned his lesson, however. The Little Man offers to exchange tails, but instead of his own, Robbut chooses the tail of a garter snake, knowing that it will not tear and be muddied. He finds it to be both beautiful and useful; he can flick it out and smack any grasshoppers that jeer at him. But this is not the case for the other rabbits, who tease him mercilessly. They are not impressed with his tail's beauty. His parents are distraught; in fact, his father sends him away because the tail suggests a rat ancestry, and he will have nothing of that. Despondent, Robbut crawls under a bush, leaving his tail across the path so that when Frank Glynn the gardener sees it, he cuts it off with a spade. In pain, Robbut rushes back to the Little Man, who gives him back his own tail.

The narrator suggests that Robbut has still not learned his lesson: "By the third day, however, he had completely forgotten about his troubles with the Cat's tail and by the fourth day he had completely forgotten about his painful experience with the Snake's tail. His memory, as the Little Man had said, was not at all good—even for a Rabbit. By the fifth day he was again dissatisfied with his own tail and on the sixth day he met the Red Fox" (62). Attracted by the beauty of the Fox's tail, Robbut rushes back to the Little Man and finds his new tail, of which he is proudest of all. The accompanying illustrations depict him holding it out proudly, like a plume; fanning himself with it; curling it around his feet and posing like a china animal; and running as it streams behind him. But like his other tails, this one will get him into trouble. Spied by the fox-hunting Hounds of the Swallowtail Hunt, he races across the countryside, knowing that he had often outstripped dogs before. But his tail throws him off balance as he crosses the stream, and it becomes sodden and heavy. It catches in briars and keeps him from squeezing into the tunnels that he could have used to escape. Thorns and barbed wire catch at it and tear out the hair, and finally, exhausted and hurt, he manages to escape under a barn, where he is saved by the farmers who evict the hunters.

In the chapter entitled "Humility," Robbut shows that he has finally learned his lesson; he is pictured with his ears back, hands clasped in prayer, and it is not hard to discern what he is praying for. The hunters have chased him out of familiar territory, and he finds it rough going, particularly with his tail: "It was cold and muddy and wet, and the trash it had picked up in the barnyard did not make it a pleasant place in which to bury one's nose" (86). He is found by the Red Deer, who takes him on his back and returns him to his own hill. He drags himself back to the Little Man's house, where he collapses. There his tail is restored, and Robbut gallops home, down through the sunset, satisfied completely at last.

The characters are familiar to those who have read *Rabbit Hill:* the woodchuck, skunk, Red Buck (now a deer), and fox all make cameo appearances, usually to move the narrative along. The rabbits are not Little Georgie and his family but much the same in their play and exuberance. Robbut's father bears a strong similiarity to the father of Little Georgie, not in his harsh judgmentalism but in the stilted formality of his speech: " 'This,' he said, 'is the most crushing blow that has ever happened to me. From time to time certain malicious gossips have spread the rumor that there was a strain of Rat blood in our family. This I have always vigorously denied and have managed to squelch all such vile suspicions. Now you must appear—obviously part Rat: Oh, the disgrace! Oh, the humiliation!' " (52–53). The elevated diction, the exclamatory tone, the rhetorical stance that seems to call attention to itself—all are elements of Father in *Rabbit Hill*. The difference in characterization between *Robbut* and *Rabbit Hill,* however, lies in the fact that in the former, the characters are only cameos; they are undeveloped and one-dimensional. Even Robbut, the protagonist, suffers from this one-dimensional treatment, for he is characterized only by a silly impulsiveness that leads to all sorts of difficulties.

Where *Robbut* fails is in its predictability: there is a fablelike quality about this fantasy that leads to an inevitability that is not striking but dull. Robbut goes through three trials until he learns his lesson: that he must be, should be, content with what he is; that he is, in fact, exactly and perfectly what he should be. The surprise lies only in the fact that he does not learn this lesson after the first trial. If the work wishes to be a fable, then it is too long and diffuse; it lacks the crispness and the concentrated action that makes the fable successful. But if it wishes to be a novel, then it lacks the depth of character and the interaction of setting, narrative, and persona that leads to a fulfilling work.

In fact, it seems that Lawson is trying to combine his Rabbit Hill books with the whimsical fantasies of books like *Mr. Twigg's Mistake, McWhinney's Jaunt,* and *Mr. Wilmer.* In each of those books, however, the humor and delight are generated by the puzzled and sometimes odd human perspective. In combining that form with the animal perspective, Lawson has mixed genres unevenly, so that Robbut's perspective seems neither human nor animal—a balance happily achieved in *Rabbit Hill* and *The Tough Winter.* Thus at the end of the story, the Little Man tells Robbut that he has the finest tail in the world—for a rabbit. Still, the Woodchuck fusses at Robbut, saying that "some people are never satisfied" (94). In fact, neither seems quite right. Robbut is either too human or not human enough; he certainly seems barely a rabbit— except in the illustrations.

If the novel can be said to be successful in any sense, it is in the merger of text and illustration. Here, more that in any other of Lawson's novels, the illustrations carry the story—in fact, they tell the story. The opening endpage illustration suggests the conflict that Robbut must deal with, and no two-page spread is without its accompanying illustration until the end of the novel, when three text-only spreads unexpectedly appear. The setting is made almost entirely the task of the illustrations; this is true both of the countryside and the house of the Little Man. But Lawson is particularly adept at marking the distinction between the tails as they are first acquired and as they are lost. In each case, the tail starts off full and elegant on a very happy and satisfied rabbit and ends wet and bedraggled and partially naked—or else cut off.

The cover illustration shows Robbut peering out from a grouping of lilies, daffodils, and lilies of the valley, supported by a grouping of mushrooms. It is the only realistic portrayal of Robbut, where his expression is not humanized to some extent. But in reducing the importance of the landscape, the context of the other animals, and the very rabbit nature of the protagonist, Lawson has stripped the story of the elements that made *Rabbit Hill* so successful. He would not make the same mistake when he came to *The Tough Winter.*

Edward, Hoppy and Joe

Robbut: A Tale of Tails was followed in 1952 by *Edward, Hoppy and Joe,* a book that is today among the rarest of Lawson's fantasies and a gap in the shelves of many a Lawson collection. Like *Robbut: A Tale of Tails, Edward, Hoppy and Joe* concerns the animals that Lawson saw all around him on Rabbit Hill, and he maintains his consistent characterization of them all. The deer here is stately, running a school for gentlefolk. The rabbits are impulsive, though Father remains the distinguished gentleman, careful with his elevated language and quite conscious of his family honor. Edward, the youngest rabbit and the protagonist, has a circle of friends similar to those of Little Georgie in *Rabbit Hill.* And the dangers the characters encounter—dogs, running water, hunger—are all ones that Lawson has examined before. *Edward, Hoppy and Joe* does not offer a new story. It is telling, in this light, that this book did not come out of Viking. Characterization may be said, kindly, to be consistent; a less kind word might be repetitive.

Like the other Rabbit Hill books, however, this one does have a structural center: it is about the education of Edward, who at the beginning of the novel is ignorant not only in the academic sense but in the instinctive needs of being a wise and canny rabbit. When Father discovers this lack, he sets out to correct it, beginning with the alphabet. Yet after that, the correction comes rather haphazardly, as Father reacts to events rather than initiates them toward Edward's training. Edward's mishaps all tend to be at first potentially disastrous but, in the end, become not particularly dangerous, as Edward is surrounded by loving friends, parents, and neighbors, and he learns quite quickly the lesson his Father is always ready to announce.

The novel opens in the house of Mr. Beaver, who is the solid neighbor, the one who can be relied on, the one who is trustworthy, the craftsman of the animal community. Father Rabbit laments the ignorance of his son, and the beaver suggests that experience might be the answer: "I wouldn't go too hard on the book learning. I never had much of it myself, just a little reading and writing and figgering, and I've gotten along pretty well. . . . Practical learning's more in my line."[8] Father does not respond to this advice, and his initial impulse is to reject it. When he begins to teach the alphabet to Edward, however, he uses those things he sees right around him—A is for apple, B for bluejay, C for clover, D for dog. All of these are intimate parts of a rabbit's life. Soon it is clear that Edward's education will come principally out of his practical experience.

The rest of the novel tells of a series of incidents in which Edward learns various lessons. He is intrigued by the danger of cars, and eventually he is threatened when he is trapped inside one. He asks for a canoe and must learn to swim first. He wishes to stay out late and learns the value of rest in his own bed. He wishes to skate and learns that rabbits are indeed limited in some things. He grows fat from eating too much dessert and finds that he cannot run as fast as a rabbit should. He takes the canoe out when he shouldn't, and spends the night unhappily when the canoe tips and the river grows too strong for him and his friends to paddle upstream. He is careless and is attacked by a copperhead.

Each of the short chapters follows the same predictable pattern and concludes with Edward didactically acknowledging the value of the lesson he has learned: "I'll never stay out late again, if I can only have my own nice bed to sleep in" (30–31), he promises. After he eats dessert once too often, he claims that "from now on I'll be satisfied with my good simple food; good old grass and clover and bark" (74). The pattern is one of testing, experiencing, and learning. This is a pattern that Little Georgie follows at times in *Rabbit Hill,* but in that novel the pattern had been combined with a strong narrative line; here the pattern *is* the narrative line.

Nevertheless, Edward learns some valuable lessons that are not so overt, not so didactic. Then greatest of these is the value of friendship. Hoppy is a toad and Joe an opossum, and each has his limitations:

Hoppy can move only very slowly, while Joe tends to faint away at any exciting moment. And yet despite their differences, they are close. They will not abandon each other; at one point Hoppy and Joe ask Edward to hurry on ahead so that he will not be in trouble with his parents; at their rate of travel, it will be three or four days before they can get back. But Edward will not leave them. During a trip "out west," Edward leads away a gray fox that is eager to capture Joe; later, Joe emerges from his sloth and leaps at a copperhead that has paralyzed Edward with terror. All the other lessons of discipline and instinct are subordinate to this one of friendship.

At the end of the novel, Lawson includes another, perhaps more subtle lesson, and one that provides the only real surprise: the fallibility, or perhaps the reality, of parents. Edward, Hoppy, and Joe have been eager to go to the circus, but Edward's mother has forbidden it; his father has agreed with her. But Edward goes, and he is thrilled by the clowns and animals and exuberance of the fairgrounds. Joe is accidentally locked into a cage, however, and Edward, remaining with his friend, is unable to free him until the next day. Then, unexpectedly, they find that Edward's father has come surreptitiously to see the circus. When they later meet and realize that each knows where the other has been, there is a kind of conspiratorial glee about their talk: "We may both have to go without our dinners," notes Father, "but it was well worth it, was it not?" (119).

Edward may not be able to articulate what he has just found out— that his father is not so much a model but a real figure—but Father is able to articulate this, and to recognize that the realization means growth for Edward. At the end of the novel, Father goes once again to Mr. Beaver's house, a completion of the frame. There he tells Mr. Beaver what Edward has learned, as well as the result of that knowledge: "The fact that his Father is not a cold model of perfection, but just a normal Rabbit like himself. We have been much closer friends ever since" (122). Mr. Beaver's response reflects his practical nature: "Reckon that's better than all the book learning there is. . . . Reckon that's the best thing of all for a young one to learn" (122).

As with the other Rabbit Hill books and the whimsical fantasies, Lawson works hard to merge the genres of fantasy and realism. Mr. Beaver, for example, is a fine craftsman and lives by a mill pond. The opening illustration shows this but shows it through picturing him in a fine stone and wood house, lounging with Father Rabbit on the upper porch. Many of the illustrations play with this merger: Uncle Phineas, a

FROM ROBERT LAWSON, *EDWARD, HOPPY AND JOE*
(NEW YORK: KNOPF, 1952).

rabbit, sleeping in a spring bed; the three friends in a canoe; Edward
doing his homework in a messy room filled with strewn paper and
chewed rose branches. And this merger is also important in the text. In
many ways Edward is quite the rabbit: in the things he eats, in his running, in his interest in garden food. But he is also quite the young child.
His usual mode of conversation with adults—until the end of the
novel—is a litany of questions that have no answers. He is fascinated by
things he should not touch, like automobiles. He is intrigued by water
and the adventure of messing around in boats. He likes cowboys and
Indians and circuses; in short, he likes to play imaginatively. Like a
child, he is fascinated by something for the moment, like roller-skates,
and then he quickly abandons it. He does not like bedtime, school, or
giving up desserts, but he recognizes that not going to bed, not going to
school, or not eating well leads to painful consequences.

This merger of fantasy and realism is right at the center of what Lawson was doing in the other Rabbit Hill books. Unfortunately *Edward,*

Hoppy and Joe repeats the pattern of the merger rather than varying or enlarging upon it. The question of Edward's education in practical life could have been a powerful centering motif, but it is diluted in the episodic quality of the chapters. There are perhaps reasons for this novel being such a rare find today.

The Tough Winter

A decade was to pass before Lawson published the sequel to *Rabbit Hill, The Tough Winter,* although he had always planned to write a sequel. "Ever since *Rabbit Hill* I've been waiting for the right idea to go ahead on," he told *Horn Book*'s Anne Carroll Moore.[9] The book came out in September 1954 to virtually the same kinds of reviews that had marked its predecessor. "Delightful," "happy," and "amusing," wrote Jennie Lindquist, the editor of *Horn Book*. "Appealing," "delightful," and a work of "charm," wrote Nancy Jane Day for the *Saturday Review of Literature*. In the *New York Times Book Review,* C. Elta Van Norman recalled the emphasis on landscape in the reviews for *Rabbit Hill:* "There is gentle humor in the book's sensitive, beautiful drawings. The prose reflects a love of nature and a feeling of respect for all small beings, in many of whom we can recognize traits of our closest human friends."[10]

The reviews are similar for good reason. The two books share much, and it is a sharing not limited to the literal level. There is the shared landscape, the shared set of characters, the shared characterizations. But beyond that is the shared thematic concern that plays through both novels—that there is enough for all to live in peace. In fact, *The Tough Winter* establishes this theme even more strongly, as it plays out through the entire plot and affects the actions of Tim McGrath, who is left wondering at the behavior of the animals and New Folks at the end of *Rabbit Hill*.

But even beyond this, the two novels share a tightness of narrative structure that is not present in Lawson's other work. Lawson's novels are, in general, marked by a loose structuring, as the author establishes a fantastic central motif—a gas that allows a bicycle to fly, a man who can talk with animals, a boy with an astonishing sense of smell—and then allows episodes to swirl around that motif, all leading to a climax that is engendered by the motif but not necessarily its culmination. In *Rabbit Hill* and *The Tough Winter,* however, Lawson creates a narrative structure that is much tighter. In *Rabbit Hill,* all episodes contribute directly to answering a single question: What are the New Folks going to be like?

In *The Tough Winter,* all episodes contribute to a different question: How are the animals going to survive the tough winter?

The novel opens with dire predictions from Uncle Analdas: this is going to be a tough winter. His predictions had not come true in the previous novel, but here he proves to be correct. In fact, there is a downward spiral of events. The news that opens *The Tough Winter* is not the advent of New Folks, but the fact that the New Folks are leaving. This means that the nightly feasts will no longer be available, and the animals scurry to bring in a harvest. The night after Thanksgiving surprises them, however; it is the night of the last feast, and the night when an ice storm blankets the Hill, trapping most of the animals in their burrows. The storm also traps Mr. Muldoon, the Folks' cat, as he sleeps by the wall, and Georgie fetches the Red Buck to free him—an escape noted with astonishment by Tim McGrath.

When the Folks leave, Caretakers come, along with their dog, whose first act is to hunt Uncle Analdas and take a bite from his left hip. The dog establishes what the narrator refers to as a Reign of Terror, and it is clear that the Caretakers are not particularly worried about his attacks on the animals; Georgie and Father are both surprised by shotgun blasts fired at them while they are looking over the remnants of the garden. It is only when Phewie the skunk attacks the dog that the menace is over; the dog remains collared outside the house by the garage, where he is taunted by the Gray Fox.

But things get worse. Fire bursts across the Hill, the result of the Caretaker's carelessness, destroying much of the fodder for the winter. What is particularly devastating for Little Georgie's family is that the fire trucks crash through the roof of their storeroom, destroying much of what had been laid aside for the winter. With such a loss, many of the animals are forced to leave, including the field mice, the fox, the Red Buck with his family. Only the animals who are asleep remain, although Georgie and his family, along with Willie Fieldmouse, are determined to hold out until spring.

There seems to be something of a respite on Christmas Eve, when Tim McGrath brings a feast to the animals—most of whom are gone. But as the snow continues to fall and Porkey comes out of his hole on Groundhog Day to see his shadow, the animals realize that things are now desperate. Mother is sent off to her daughter's home, and Uncle Analdas seems to be going crazy. Soon he disappears, and only later do the animals learn where he has gone: he has set off for the "Bluegrass Country," where the Folks have gone. He only makes it to Tim McGrath's barn, where he settles into the warm hay. But Father goes to look for him, and in so doing, becomes sick. Georgie, alone now with Willie on the Hill, is clearly starving, and the illustration shows every rib.

But then, one day, Willie and Little Georgie look out of the burrow and it is raining, a warm spring rain. The snow melts quickly, and the grass is luscious and green: Father revives, Mother returns, the Caretakers drive away, and the Folks come back, bowing their hats to Willie and Georgie. That night a meal is set out for them. The return of the Folks is heralded around the countryside, and soon all the animals are rushing back to their old homes—to the astonishment of Tim McGrath. When Uncle Analdas returns, he has decided to travel to his Bluegrass Country every winter, but Georgie and Willie resolve to always remain on the Hill "and fight the winter through."[11]

Perhaps the most striking element of this sequel is the radiating circles of kindness that the Folks have inspired on Rabbit Hill; at the end of *Rabbit Hill,* Tim McGrath had been astonished at how the animals had preserved the garden on the Hill and bemused by the feasts that the Folks had spread each night. But in this novel, even he is caught up in this circle. When Mr. Muldoon is trapped by the ice storm, it is the mice who go against their nature to bring the news to the rabbits. The mice prevail upon Foxy to go against his nature and yield some of the turkey carcass he has taken; they bring the meat to Mr. Muldoon. The rabbits encourage the Red Buck to go against his nature to come free the cat. And Tim McGrath, seeing this, brings food for the animals—this against his own nature: "He went to the toolhouse, gathered a huge armful of hay, and lugged it up the Hill to the edge of Pine Wood, where he spread it out beside the Deer's trail. 'Feedin' the wild stock!' He laughed at himself a bit sheepishly. 'I must be gettin' soft in the head. Next thing I'll take to readin' books'" (38). It is a giant leap for McGrath to come to this point; he had been the one to advise traps and poison earlier. But come Christmas, he repeats the feast, and this time he recalls the stance of the New Folks: "Tim emerged, staggering under the weight of a huge forkful of hay. He carried it up the Hill to where the statue of St. Francis, swathed in burlap and knee-deep in snow, rose grayly against the dark pines. Three forkfuls he carried up, until there was a long pile of hay spreading its sweetness on the still, crisp air. . . . There was a basket of grain, another of nuts, cakes of seed-studded suet, a cake of salt. There were pungent red apples, crips carrots, fresh lettuce leaves. Then, as a crowning touch, Tim brought from the car a generous panful of bones—chop bones, steak bones, turkey bones" (81). The Christmas Eve feast comes from Tim

McGrath's initiation, not that of the New Folks. His care for the animals and his evident pleasure in them mirror that of the Folks, however. It prepares the reader for Tim's berating of the Caretaker when he shoots at Little Georgie and Father. And it explains his kindness to Uncle Analdas, as he allows him to sit out the winter in his warm barn.

Certainly there had been kindness among the animals; Father has led dogs away from the Gray Fox, and in *The Tough Winter* Little Georgie protects Porkey the woodchuck from the dog digging down toward him. But what is remarkable about the kindness exhibited in *The Tough Winter* is how it calls the giver so far from his nature. The lesson of the New Folks is an urging of benevolence that goes beyond natural inclination—even beyond instinct.

The antithesis of the kindness, however, is suggested by the ironically named Caretakers. Their first act is to loose their dog upon Uncle Analdas; they later shoot at the rabbits and set fire to the Hill. But their stance toward the animals is suggested even more forcefully by their absence. They never appear outside the house; their presence is suggested only by the yellow light in the kitchen. Unable and unwilling to participate in the life of the countryside around them, they are barred from its pleasures; they do not see the procession of the animals around Saint Francis. When they drive away, they leave "without even a backward glance" (115); when the Folks return, they stop in the driveway to greet Willie and Little Georgie—"Good Morning, sirs, and good luck to you" (119)—and resolve to tend to the animals before anything else: "Goodness, the poor things look half-starved. . . . Tim must set out a good meal for them" (119).

As with *Rabbit Hill,* the endpages of *The Tough Winter* say much about the novel's narrative action and establish the landscape of that action. As with the endpages for *Rabbit Hill,* Lawson depicts the wide Connecticut landscape, with the stone house at the center. But whereas the former illustration depicts a busy, energetic landscape, this illustration shows one covered with snow; there is a distinct sense of stillness about the picture, as the stars glisten down on a frozen hill. Snow covers everything except for the still evergreens and three rosebushes that poke their way up. The only movement is in the lower right corner, as Willie Fieldmouse and Little Georgie head back to the burrow, loaded with clippings from the rose bushes, the moon throwing their shadows in front of them. The stillness and quiet suggest the kind of frozen atmosphere that will mark the narrative. The emptiness also suggests the emptiness of the Hill—a distinct difference between *Rabbit Hill* and *The Tough*

Winter. It introduces as well the harsh conditions that will set the narrative and the anthropomorphism of the animals. It is not an illustration, however, that suggests the strict boundaries of Rabbit Hill; the Hill seems more open and limitless, an important consideration for the novel, as so many of the characters leave.

In fact, this leave-taking is thematically important. As one by one the animals depart, Father and Mother, Uncle Analdas, and Little Georgie and Willie Fieldmouse become more and more determined to stay on, to see the winter through. When Mother is sent away, Uncle Analdas travels to what he thinks is Bluegrass Country, and Father becomes ill; life turns quite difficult for Little Georgie: "There came an evening when Little Georgie thought he had reached the limit of his endurance. Father was worse than ever. Between coughing spells he mumbled and rambled on about his youth in the Bluegrass, about Uncle Analdas, about Mother, about Porkey. Then he would relapse into long periods of silence, his harsh breathing the only sign of life. Little Georgie was in despair" (112). Father is revived by his instinctive sense that the weather has changed. But what is remarkable in all this is that Little Georgie never thinks for a moment about leaving the Hill; neither, for that matter, does Father, despite his illness.

Little Georgie's concluding affirmation that he would always stay and fight the winter through is an affirmative of home. Certainly this theme had been a part of *Rabbit Hill,* but it is even stronger here, for now this is a home that must be fought for. And once the fight has been successful, there is a sense of joy as the snow melts off, a sense that home—in all its fullness—has been reestablished. If much of children's literature is about establishing home, here is a novel about an established home that is threatened, then affirmed through the willingness of characters to persist. The result is an Edenic world of water and green grass: "Except for few soggy patches of white under the evergreens where the snow had been deepest, the earth was completely clear, steaming under the warm sun. The winter-long snow blanket had preserved the grass, the lawns were quite green, penciled here and there by wandering brown lines that marked the courses of Willie's now vanished tunnels. Tiny rivulets of water ran everywhere. The ground was a soaking sponge, from the river came a steady rushing roar. The layer of steam rising from the earth whiled and eddied lazily in the gentle stir of air flowing up from the south" (116–17). The images of warm refreshment dominate here, becoming poignant because the animals have struggled to survive for just this time.

It would be easy to convert the novel into a didactic parable. In fact, the language of the summary of *Rabbit Hill* that opens *The Tough Winter* takes on the tone of a parable:

> *There was a Hill, and on the Hill there was a house known as the Big House. The Folks who lived in the Big House loved and respected all Animals, and the Small Animals who lived on the Hill loved and trusted their Folks—and were not afraid. . . .*
>
> *But peace and happiness do not always flow on endlessly, without interruption, and Folks are not trees, to stay forever rooted in one spot. So it came to pass . . .* (10)

The diction is stately, an effect created by the repetition, the slow rhythm, and the parallel structures. Visual effect is aided by setting the summary in italics. The first impression of this piece is to suggest that the work will convey moral lessons; it will be, in short, a beast fable.

But Lawson indicates early on that he will have none of that. The opening line of the first chapter suggests a totally different narrative stance: "Uncle Analdas, the old, old Rabbit, glared around at his cronies" (11). The concern with repetition and parallelism is lost; the narrator is direct, declarative. The character is humanized, the action instantaneous. In fact, Analdas is about to prophesy a tough winter, so that the novel's principal narrative action is immediately introduced. In short, what Lawson is concerned with here is story; he never lets the potential didacticism of the piece take control, and he does this by focusing on the characters' ways of coping with the tough winter, as well as their condition, rather than focusing on interior ruminations about the nature of survival. The characters act rather than ruminate—and, of course, they are animals, and this is appropriate.

The novel succeeds not because of the weight of its meaning but because of its cast of characters and, particularly, its tight narrative plot line. This is in fact a survival story, as first provisions are depleted, then supporting adults disappear until at last Little Georgie and Willie Field-mouse are left on their own to struggle through the winter. The struggle, however, affirms more strongly than anything else their ties to home; the day may come when George, like his sisters, leaves the burrow, but it has not come yet. Time has diminished Little Georgie's memory of the difficulties of the winter, but it has not diminished his appreciation for his home; he will not go with Uncle Analdas to Bluegrass Country, not because he enjoys the winter struggle but because he is, childlike, inextricably tied to home.

Chapter Five
The Whimsical Nonsense Tales

Even as Robert Lawson was writing his historical fantasies, he began work on a quintet of books that explored the parameters of yet another genre: nonsense. As with his historical fantasies, however, Lawson presses the boundaries of the genre. In his historical fantasies, he had combined historical situations with fantasy by endowing the narrative with an animal narrator. In these nonsense works, he is again combining the real with the fantastic, in that each juxtaposes realistic characters who face recognizable difficulties with absurd, nonsensical situations such as a giant mole, or an impossibly developed sense of smell, or the ability to talk with animals. Here again, as with the historical fantasies, it is the interplay of the realistic with the nonsensical or fantastic that generates much of the narrative action. Unfortunately that interplay, generally, was not strong enough to center the action and development of the novels, which, with the exception of *The Fabulous Flight,* are marked by loose structures, underdeveloped characters, inconsistent tones, and confused stances.

Mr. Wilmer

Mr. Wilmer (1945), like Lawson's other nonsense novels, revolves around a single bit of nonsense stretched tightly and spun out through the course of the narrative. Here the nonsense is Mr. Wilmer's sudden ability to make noises back in the depths of his throat and then be able to talk with—and understand—animals. Unlike his other nonsense works, here Lawson does not focus on the genesis of the ability; in *McWhinney's Jaunt* there would be the discovery of Z-Gas to spur the action on, and in *Mr. Twigg's Mistake* there would be Vitamin X to generate the narrative action. Here, however, the nonsense will be left to stand by itself.

It is, on the one hand, an unfortunate start to this novel. Hugh Lofting's Dr. Dolittle novels had preceded *Mr. Wilmer* by some 25 years; in fact, they were still being written and quite popular. Lawson must have foreseen that any book that involved a character talking to animals must inevitably be compared with these, which had established a world—

Puddleby-on-the-Marsh—within which it seemed right and appropriate that animals could speak to a gentle doctor who had learned their language out of fascination and kindness. But here Lawson sets up no such context; it all happens abruptly and unexpectedly and readers have little chance to set aside their disbelief.

On the other hand, however, Lawson is doing something quite different from Lofting; he is not particularly interested in creating a full fantasy world with its own inner cohesion. In a sense he is out for a lark by asking himself, "What if a meek and mild character suddenly could speak to animals?" He prefaces the novel with a quote that would be completely out of place in the more serious Dolittle books—"The most useless day of all is that in which we have not laughed"[1]—and this quote seems to hang over the narrative. This is all a lark, something readers are to be laughing at. (A novel with this purpose would perhaps not be unwelcome at the end of four long years of war.)

As with several of Lawson's nonsense books, audience is here a real question. *Mr. Wilmer* was marketed by Little, Brown as a child's book, and certainly the illustrations all lend themselves to that market. But in fact not a single child appears in the novel—although there are certainly moments when a child would have been appropriate. The problems that Mr. Wilmer faces are in fact adult problems: a dull life, a boring job, a search for a vocation, recognizing and reacting to romantic love, marriage and the establishment of a home. A listing like this suggests that a child's market is inappropriate.

Still, Lawson's work is difficult to pigeonhole. Mr. Wilmer is an adult, but his responses to the adult world around him are only childlike. He always seems under the thumb of authority that appears imperious and solid, and, until late in the novel, he cannot even conceive of confronting it. He is unable to deal with any business and keeps his voluminous accounts in shoeboxes—until another adult can put his affairs in order. He seems more comfortable around animals than around the competent adults who surround him. In fact, it is these competent adults— benign and affable, fortunately—who guide all of Mr. Wilmer's stunning affairs so that he will not be completely overwhelmed.

Even his marriage is childlike. This same group of adults must guide him to the proposal, for he, like a child, is unable to see beyond superficialities. The wedding is almost a play, and certainly the procession to the new home—where another set of guardian adults is waiting to take care of him—is more a circus than the opening of a honeymoon. Although the narrator suggests that Mr. Wilmer grows physically through the narrative—a fact supported by the illustrations—he hardly seems to grow emotionally. He remains the child and thus, enigmatically, close to the child reader even as he deals with adult situations—a delicate balance.

Mr. Wilmer opens with its protagonist discovering almost to his surprise that it is his twenty-ninth birthday, a time of both endings and potential beginnings. But little of note seems to happen. Mr. Wilmer will work through his expected routine on the way to a job that consists of nothing more than adding and subtracting figures, a job whose one joy is the sight of Miss Sweeney and whose constant difficulty is the presence of Mr. Twitch, whose look and name seem to suggest that he is one of *The Wizard of Oz*'s munchkins writ large. Everything proceeds precisely as Mr. Wilmer anticipates, except for two oddities. First, the policeman whom he has passed every day will not let him feed his horse a Peppermint Patootie, and, second, he hears a small voice berate the policeman: "The big, bullnecked, ham-faced, overbearing bully, . . . the stupid, selfish, heavy-bottomed brute! I'll get even with him, I'll fix him—" (8). These are words that Mr. Wilmer would himself never use, but there is no one else around to use them either. It is, in fact, his first inkling of animal language.

At noon one April Saturday Mr. Wilmer finishes work and resolves to do something unusual: he will go to the zoo on Saturday afternoon rather than his usual Sunday. There he sees Toby, a lion, and discovers that he can both understand and speak to him. Toby is suffering from a dreadful toothache, something all the specialists are unable to diagnose. The Zoo Keeper Gallagher escorts him out, but the next day when Mr. Wilmer returns to check on Toby, the Keeper pounces on him and brings him to Mr. Carrington-Carr, the cultured and suave director of the zoo. With Mr. Wilmer's help they locate Toby's difficult tooth. Mr. Carrington-Carr then tours the zoo with Wilmer, a record book in his hand, asking Wilmer to interview each of the animals to find out where it is from and the circumstances under which it came to the zoo. Wilmer's accuracy convinces Mr. Carrington-Carr that he has the gift of animal speech.

The sensation caused by the story in the newspapers the following morning leads to Wilmer's being fired from the safe, sane, and colossal insurance company, something Miss Sweeney congratulates him on; Wilmer, however, finds himself with no employment, fearing that he will turn into one of the bedraggled tramps he sees on a park bench. But there is no fear of this, as soon he has more offers and more employment than he knows what to do with. He is hired as "Special Animal Consultant to the Central Zoo" (60), a task that involves speaking with and caring for the animals' needs at a salary quadrupling what he had made before. He is beset by potential managers, by autograph seekers, by those wishing his name for endorsements, and even by Mrs. Plushington, who puts him on a fabulous retainer so that he will come and speak with her pampered poodle.

His finances expand beyond his ability to imagine, and his life seems to open up. He is quite happy at the zoo, although quite busy. He resolves to interview all of the animals to see if they are content, something that he is also asked to do at other zoos around the country. Under the wing of Mr. Carrington-Carr, he learns to deal with endorsements and pressures, and soon Wilmer grows in confidence and self-reliance. He is appointed "Special Deputy Commissioner of Police" to watch over the mounted patrol and is accorded a place with chief dignitaries during a parade—something he could never have imagined happening before. The same policeman who once hollered at him for feeding his horse now salutes him.

But Wilmer's endorsements and requests and financial offers continue to grow, and at Mr. Carrington-Carr's suggestion Wilmer hires Miss Sweeney, whom he has never forgotten, as his personal secretary. She comes in a burst of flowers, enlivening Zoo Keeper Gallagher and everyone else at the zoo. (Wilmer had sent an old-fashioned set of flowers to Mrs. Keeler, who runs his boardinghouse, and a modern corsage to Miss Sweeney, but he had mixed them up by getting the addresses wrong. As it turns out, however, old-fashioned flowers are precisely what Miss Sweeney cherishes. Mr. Wilmer is fortunate yet again.) Miss Sweeney arranges all of Wilmer's finances, straightens out his scheduling, and helps him to prepare a series of animal interviews he has been asked to write for a city magazine.

Mr. Wilmer's life begins to change the Keelers' boardinghouse where he stays, making it a joyful, raucous place, filled with flowers. Miss Sweeney moves in, as does Walter, a seal in need of some quiet from his busy circus life. He plays his trumpet for them, and they dance through the evenings. More and more Wilmer is entranced by Miss Sweeney, but he is unable to articulate what this means for him: "Never in his life had William Wilmer had fun like this and never in his life had he seen anything so fascinating as the way Miss Sweeney's mop of coppery hair swung about her face and shoulders when she whirled and spun, or heard anything so lovely as her gay ringing laughter" (169). But he does not acknowledge any of this to her.

Once again Mr. Carrington-Carr steps in and suggests that Wilmer might buy a farm; it is an especially good idea because some of the animals—such as Lucy the elephant—could find it a place to relax, and the Keelers would be eager to go live on a farm. Wilmer, about to tour the zoos of the country, leaves it all to Miss Sweeney, who finds a beautiful old farmhouse with several wings and surrounding fields for the animals, all at the foot of a hill, at the top of which sits a large barn. Wilmer is eager to move, but on the day he cannot understand everyone's unease. Finally the Keelers tell him what is patently obvious to everyone but Wilmer: Miss Sweeney cannot in all propriety move out to the farmhouse with him unless they are married.

Finally Wilmer is able to hope and to act. Using his status as deputy police commissioner, he has the police search for her—she has fled the boardinghouse—but it is he himself who finds her at the zoo. He proposes; they are married in a whirlwind; then atop Lucy, they make their way to the farm, still, it seems, two children on a lark.

Mr. Wilmer is actually a novel about emergence. It is not so much a novel about growth or maturation, for these characters always seem to be playing at being adult. It is more about the leaving behind of restricting circumstances and opening into new possibilities of action. Some of these new possibilities are obviously fantasies, but some are quite real and, beneath the gentle humor, represent real yearnings.

The vision of *Metropolis* that Lawson will later conjure up in *Mr. Twigg's Mistake* is in *Mr. Wilmer* more dreadful in that Mr. Wilmer seems so unaware that he does not have to live his life according to the predictable routine that has bound him; at least Mr. Twigg has the luxurious fiction of believing that his work is meaningful. Wilmer does not have this. His unvarying routine deadens him, so that he can hardly recognize, much less respond to, love when it comes upon him. He imagines himself as one of the animals in the zoo: "They were so powerful and lithe, yet so resigned to being shut up in cages. Somehow he felt a great kinship with them" (16). He feels this especially toward Toby the lion, "for of all the animals he seemed the handsomest and most resigned. All day he lay with his proud yellow eyes staring fixedly into space, contemptuous alike of old ladies' poking umbrellas or children's tossed candies" (17). But this is deception, just as much as his daydreaming about going on cruises to exotic places, perhaps even with

Miss Sweeney. He is neither powerful nor lithe nor handsome, although he is resigned to his little cage.

Much of the novel's humor centers on how Wilmer overcomes his closed in, caged situation; his approach is exactly the unexpected: he does nothing, or virtually nothing. Circumstances, events, and characters act on Wilmer and shape him, rather than the other way around. In fact, his emergence is a kind of collective effort, involving Miss Sweeney, Director Carrington-Carr, the Keelers, Zoo Keeper Gallagher, and virtually anyone Wilmer comes into contact with, including Mrs. Plushington, who helps him to see certain possibilities in his own life. Each of these characters pushes him in certain directions that will eventually lead to a vocation and romantic happiness.

And, of course, the principal plot situation of animal language is itself not of Mr. Wilmer's making. It, too, comes upon him unexpectedly, a gift for which he has no expectation or preparation on his birthday. The arrival of animal language prepares Wilmer for his emergence, but the way it arrives also suggests how much the nonhero Wilmer truly is. Although initiating nothing, Wilmer is initiated into life. It is this humorous paradox that Lawson plays with and expands.

This pattern works itself out in concentric circles. It begins with Wilmer's discovery of animal language—a purely idiosyncratic and individual discovery. Nothing he does initiates this discovery; it just comes to him on an April day. That, however, leads to his being discovered by the zookeeper, which then leads to his being discovered by the zoo director, which then leads to his being discovered by a group of scientists. From here he is fired from his first job, brought into his second, introduced into various new positions, and finally introduced into romantic love and marriage—all with almost no initiative on his part. Carried along on the wave of the fantasy, Wilmer emerges from his patterned life into a full, rich, and somewhat unpredictable new life. The humor of the book lies in following the wave (and not, as one might expect, the animal language) and watching Wilmer flounder toward wholeness in front of it.

One aspect of this emergence is the movement from the city into the country; in Lawson's work this is always a healthy movement. The country is the place of joy, serenity, and fullness, a place where anything can happen; moles can grow larger than a person, and tough winters can be faced in innovative ways. In the city is discomfort (Lucy the elephant can never find the proper mudpool for her feet) and humdrum routine. Wilmer can never really anticipate any change in his routine, which is marked by its lack of beauty: "The bus took him seven blocks crosstown and twelve down, to the subway station. At the newsstand there, just as every morning, he bought his copy of the *Daily Bleat* and a roll of Peppermint Patooties. On the subway train he sat in his regular front right-hand corner seat of the fourth car, took one Peppermint Patootie, and looked at the pictures of murderers, gunmen and politicians, as far as 72nd Street" (5–6). The vista is almost nonexistent, and he focuses on things that have little to do with him. But that patterning is like a cocoon in that it opens up into the country, which is foreshadowed by the frequent references to flowers associated with the zoo, Mrs. Keeler, and especially Miss Sweeney. But it is particularly apparent in the description of the farm that Mr. and Mrs. Wilmer are to occupy:

> Below them the setting sun flooded the valley with a light that seemed almost a golden mist. In a slight hollow lay a broad stone and white shingled house, sheltered by towering elms and maples, their dark shadows striping across emerald green lawns. Up behind the house a great red barn reared its bulk like a protecting medieval fortress.
>
> They saw details: a thin column of blue smoke rising from one of the many chimneys, the meandering course of a willow-shaded brook, the gleam of a pond, a purple-blue fog of lilacs by the kitchen, a tall slender pear tree clad in white blossoms. (214)

The accompanying illustration (214–15) depicts the stone house faithfully, setting its several wings and enormous barn all by themselves in a gently rolling valley that the chapter title has named Arcady—an accurate name from both the perspectives of the animals who will come to live there and the Wilmers.

It is, of course, animal language that has finally brought Wilmer to this place, and if he seems somewhat overwhelmed, he recognizes that here is deep comfort and security, a solid home for the first time in his adult life. In fact, he is hardly able to believe the reality of the house: "Goodness gracious. . . this isn't—this can't all be—ours?" (217). It is a telling question. His inability to follow the wave of circumstances marks him as still something of a child. But the last hesitant word of the question—"ours"—suggests an emergence from a pattern that has brought him to a wholeness, whether or not he recognizes it by the narrative's end.

Mr. Twigg's Mistake

Two years after *Mr. Wilmer*, Lawson published *Mr. Twigg's Mistake* (1947). Despite the title of this short novel, Mr. Twigg plays only a minimal part in the narrative action, and perhaps this anomaly is indicative of the confusion that lies behind this, one of Lawson's most flawed books. On the one hand this book wants to be a satiric attack on the pretensions of the scientific community; on the other it purports to be a boy-and-his-pet story, although its ending is one of the least satisfying one might find in this genre. And in yet another sense this is an exploration of family relationships under extraordinary circumstances—with a similarly unsatisfactory conclusion.

As with *McWhinney's Jaunt,* the novel turns on a fantastic scientific blip: the extraordinary growing powers of Vitamin X provides the impetus for the narrative action. But whereas Professor McWhinney's Z-Gas works well to propel the narrative, in *Mr. Twigg's Mistake* Lawson seems unsure of what to do with his scientific blip. By the end of the novel a boy, a professor, and a mole have all experienced its effects, but there is no real conclusion to the blip. Lawson seems to have created an intriguing situation that he could not resolve, and this shows in the unsettled conclusion.

The novel begins with a satiric attack on the pretensions of scientists. Mr. Twigg is just a factotum working for a cereal company; his job is merely to mix the ingredients in Bita-Vita. But he feels that it is a highly skilled and scientific job, and he considers himself a scientist. But one day he fails to mix the cereal properly, and all the Vitamin X for thousands of boxes of cereal plunges into a single box—a box that finds its way through a series of accidents to the house of Arthur Amory Appleton, or Squirt, who has just returned from boarding school for the summer holidays—a technique Lawson would use again in *Smeller Martin.*

When Squirt finds a tiny mole, he decides to keep it for a pet, mostly because he is so bored. His father is decidedly unhelpful in suggesting what the mole might eat, and Squirt settles on several flakes of the Bita-Vita cereal, not realizing that his is a most unusual box. He too tastes the cereal, and together they fall asleep. They both begin to grow, a fact noted by Squirt's father that night when he sees Squirt's extended cuffs and when they find that General de Gaulle—the mole is named after the French general who led the Underground—has doubled in size. Squirt resolves to eat no more of the cereal, but the General will eat nothing but it.

Squirt begins a notebook of "Interesting Tricks I Have Taught General de Gaulle," and thus begins a summer of adventure with the ever-growing mole.[2] The General becomes enormously affectionate with Squirt, and they play games around the grounds, the mole tunneling underground and pretending to be an escaping prisoner. As the weeks go by, the family is astonished at the General's growth, especially when he exceeds the size of the largest known mole. But no one is more astonished than Uncle Amory, a naturalist, who resolves to write a paper about the General and takes all sorts of scientific measurements and photographs to document the General's rapid growth. He comes to believe that the mole really belongs to science and should be held in a zoo, but this the family steadfastly refuses to agree to, and Uncle Amory eventually gives in.

Meanwhile Squirt and the General continue to play their way through the summer. Uncle Amory brings Squirt an expensive arrow, which Squirt names Excalibur. Unfortunately he shoots it into the garden of the neighbor Mr. Snarple, who is, in the words of Squirt's mother, "an impossible little creature" (57). Mr. Snarple, enraged, goes to break the arrow, but as he reaches for it seems to be pulled into the ground, and of course it is the General who has dug underneath it and who brings it safely back to the Appleton property. Frustrated, Mr. Snarple sets the dog warden upon the Appletons, but of course he can find no sign of any dog; the General has learned that when strangers come he must burrow into one of his tunnels.

Squirt's father slowly comes to appreciate the services of the General. First the mole plows up the garden for him, while Squirt rakes it out. "A splendidly efficient system," he remarks, "made quite perfect by the fact that there seems no place in it reserved for me" (74). Later the General is able to save the furnace and much of the basement by digging a drain. But as he becomes more beloved by the larger family, he also comes into some danger. He will eat nothing but the cereal, and his food supply is running out. He will not eat from another box, and when the original box is thrown out Uncle Amory insists that they retrieve every flake, for he is unable to bring any pressure to bear upon the Bita-Vita cereal company, which refuses to acknowledge Mr. Twigg's mistake and refuses to release any information on the mysterious Vitamin X.

The mole by now is larger than Squirt and is causing some problems in the neighborhood. The drain he has dug for the basement has led to a flood in Mr. Snarple's garden. In addition, the mole has been stealing Mr. Snarple's watermelons. He is sighted by various other neighbors, at least one of whom begins to fear a bear in the neighborhood. He is eating more, but the food supply is now almost gone. And there is the additional problem that Squirt is scheduled to return to boarding school soon, the summer having come to an end.

All of these problems are resolved when the General apparently causes an oil geyser on the Appleton property. The geyser brings wealth to Squirt, but it also blows the General up into the sky, where he disappears in a shower of oil. The accompanying illustration suggests that he is unhurt and now digging among the stars; in any case Squirt has lost his pet, and Uncle Amory the subject of his paper. "To Discover an Oil Well" (142), Squirt notes, is the General's last trick of all.

The ending of the novel is particularly unsatisfying; it comes to a dead stop more than to a resolution. When the General's presence comes to be a problem—the summer and food supply both coming to an end simultaneously—he simply disappears into the sky, a fantastic and unexpected ending that leaves questions unfulfilled. What, for example, is the reaction of the scientific community to the reports on the mole? How does the cereal company exploit the property of its Vitamin X? How does Squirt react to the disappearance of the mole? (He seems mostly confused and irresolute.) Where has the oil come from, since geysers are unknown in Connecticut? And most confusing of all, what has happened to the mole? The illustrations seem to suggest that he is flying about the atmosphere, but there is also a suggestion that he has been blown to pieces. If the former is true, why has he not landed and found his way back? His disappearance avoids the unhappiness and poignancy of a death scene (which would have been inappropriate in a novel with such a light tone), but it also avoids any logical and reasonable resolution that brings the relationship between Squirt and the General to a satisfying and fit conclusion.

Part of the difficulty in *Mr. Twigg's Mistake* is the confusion of purposes. Much of the novel is given over to an attack on scientific arrogance and pretension, but the attack barely fits within the confines of the narrative action. This attack is first leveled at Mr. Twigg, clearly a self-important fellow who believes his company's advertising and longs to be the scientist he pretends himself to be. Uncle Amory is also a part of the satiric attack on the scientific community. He is a sort of bumbler, unable to play bridge, not above stealing watermelons, unable to figure out an appropriate present for his nephew, intemperately enthusiastic about science, old-fashioned in his sports, and rather inarticulate. And Lawson is also interested in attacking the effects of advertising, which are in part shown in Mr. Twigg, who cannot admit his mistake because his company insists that everything is done so scientifically. But the large attack comes in the success of the cereal, which has sold widely even though it is made up only of "toasted peanut shells, corn silk and coffee grounds (for that tangy, exotic, Pan-American flavor)" (4). They are advertised by "most of the stars of stage, screen and radio, as well as the better baseball players, skating, tennis, Ping-Pong and chess champions" (4).

And this seems a large difficulty with the novel: a confusion of audience. In a boy-and-his-pet story, it seems logical and likely that the perspective will be that of the boy; at least the focus will be on this relationship, the point of view generally being that of the boy. But this is not the case here; in fact, generally the boy is being observed from the outside, so that the reader rarely senses much about the relationship between Squirt and the General. Perhaps this is part of the reason the ending is not particularly poignant, as the reader has not been privy to much of the relationship and has no real feeling of loss. This confusion of purpose and audience makes *Mr. Twigg's Mistake* an unsuccessful novel. It seems to constantly revert to the adult world and its perception of events; the result is a loss of the perspective of the child world, and a distancing of the child reader. This is a difficulty that is overwhelming.

The Fabulous Flight

Of Lawson's five whimsical fantasies, the most successful was *The Fabulous Flight* (1949), the story of young Peter Peabody Pepperell III. Like E. B. White's *Stuart Little,* which was published four years earlier, *The Fabulous Flight* is about a child who becomes the size of a mouse. In fact, he grows normally until his seventh year, when he suddenly begins to grow smaller until he is only a few inches tall. Herein lies the story's central fantasy, although it has the additional fantasy of Peter's ability to speak with animals, recalling Lawson's *Mr. Wilmer.*

The distinctions between *The Fabulous Flight* and Lawson's other whimsical fantasies are legion. Here the fantasy gives rise to and supports the central narrative action; in Lawson's other works, the fantasy *is* the narrative action, often leading to a series of merely episodic and sometimes repetitive plot situations. The protagonist of *The Fabulous Flight* is a boy, rather than the adults of *Mr. Wilmer* or *McWhinney's Jaunt,* and this boy has an engaging and humorous—even a loving—relationship with the animal friend, a relationship that Lawson develops far beyond the similar relationship depicted in *Mr. Twigg's Mistake.* The structure is a strong one, centered on a quest, although the undertaking of that quest allows Lawson to have his charcters meander around Europe as McWhinney meanders around America. Nevertheless the ful-

filling of that quest, the complications it involves, and the plot situations it calls up all give the novel a greater sense of wholeness, complete-
ness, and purpose than any of Lawson's other works of this type.

The novel begins with the introduction of Peter, a normal seven-year-
old, and his father, who works in the State Department but whose
greatest love is the workshop in one wing of the house, where he and
Peter build scale models of railroads, ships, and cannon. (This dual interest later becomes important in the narrative, for it establishes the situation of the quest and explains the craftsmanship that will later be called
for.) When Peter begins to shrink, his parents are at first baffled, but
soon both they and Peter accept the situation, and over several years he
shrinks to the size of a mouse. The family seems to accept this shrinkage
as a matter of course. Soon, most of his friends are small animals, as
other children his age do not know what to make of him.

Peter is soon a great help around his father's workshop, building
models with such dexterity that they are quite lifelike. He builds a ship
to sail and small uniforms and accouterments for an animal corps so that
they can pass on parade, Peter at their head on Buck, the rabbit. When
he meets Gus, the seagull, Peter finds that he can fly; their first flight
takes him to the top of the Washington Monument. It is this last adventure that leads his father to wonder if Peter might be of help to the State
Department.

Peter is eager to tell his family about his flight, but when he returns
home he finds Mr. Pepperell quite worried; a scientist in an unknown
European country has developed a bomb so dreadful that it dwarfs the
power of the nuclear bomb. He lives on an island, blackmailing his own
country and surrounded by that country's army, who fear that someone
else will attack and wrest the secret from him. The threat, explains
Peter's father, is to civilization itself. Peter immediately sees the possibilities, and he suggests flying to that country with Gus to steal the secret.
His father, at first reluctant, agrees that the risk is worth taking, but the
Secretary of State is not convinced; only after Gus and Peter demon-
strate their abilities by sneaking into his Washington office does he
agree.

Thus begins the fabulous flight. Peter's father constructs a compartment that will ride on Gus's back; it recalls a Pullman car, although it is
complete with lockers, a bunk, and food and water storage; Peter is
more than comfortable. He is given a single weapon: a sword with a
hypodermic needle that will render anyone instantly unconscious. He is
also given tiny maps, provided by the State Department.

The journey is part quest, part tour. Peter and Gus fly north, past the colorful boardwalks of New Jersey, to the top of the Statue of Liberty, and even to Yankee Stadium, where they fly by an astonished Joe DiMaggio. They sleep overnight in Nantucket and then take "the long hop,"[3] by which Gus means the flight across the Atlantic. This is not an easy trek, and they must sleep on the ocean overnight. They battle airplanes, fly over the *Queen Mary* for pastries, endure a sudden squall, and finally arrive in London, where they land at the American embassy and are greeted joyfully. Each embassy knows only part of the top-secret mission, so here Peter is only given the identity of the scientist and shown a fuzzy photograph of him. Gus finds London disagreeable—foggy and dank—so he is gladdened when they are next sent to Copenhagen, where they learn that their destination is the tiny country of Zargonia. In Paris they are shown the layout of the scientist's castle and learn that the lake surrounding it is frequented by seagulls, so there will be little chance that they will be detected. Finally, they fly to the scientist's castle.

Peter quickly finds his way inside the study and hides behind a bookshelf; fortuitously, the safe in which the single grain of explosive is held is on the same shelf. He discovers that the scientist has in fact died, and that his place has been taken by a disguised American thug, who is forcing Zargonia to pay him gold each month and who plans to flee once he has a million dollars in gold. Officials from Zargonia are nervously complying, although keeping their army around the lake. Meanwhile, the thug, Fisheye, has brought an accomplice into the scheme, Lumps Gallagher, and together they plot their escape.

Peter settles in behind the books; he cannot think of a way into the safe. But one night, Lumps decides to ditch his partner, steal the capsule, and blackmail not one little country but the world. Peter stands by while Lumps opens the safe, and when he sees the opportunity, he plunges his hypodermic sword into Lumps' wrist, stunning him. Peter grabs the capsule, finds his way to the window ledge and the waiting Gus, and takes off, but not before Fisheye comes into the room and fires several shots at them, leading to a barrage of fire from the Zargonian forces.

Gus and Peter head on home, but decide that, since they are in Europe, they should see the sights. They travel to Venice but conclude that the roads must make living there awkward. Florence they skip as mostly art galleries. Rome is a disappointment, as most of the buildings are in ruins: "It's a wonder they wouldn't do somethin' about 'em. Peo-

ple comin' from halfway around the world to see these things and them
half tumbled down. It's a gyp game, that's what it is" (130). They are
somewhat appeased by the Vatican, but finally conclude that it would
be best to return and tell the State Department that the threat is over.

As they start over the Atlantic, Peter has an sudden insight: "I've
been thinking about that capsule. We've got it and nobody else can get
it and I don't think we ought to give it to anyone—even our own Government. It's just too terrible" (133). They resolve to dump it in the
Atlantic and Gus flies high, so high that Peter needs his oxygen mask,
before Peter drops it. Gus then plummets at an angle, speeding miles
and miles away from the blast, but even so the shock waves catch them
and destroy the compartment; Peter and Gus are blown apart, and Peter
slams into the ocean, though he is saved by the air in his flying suit. Gus
finds him floating and together they rush westward, since now there is
no food and no water to keep them. They barely make it to San Sal-
vador, retracing the route of Columbus, and after resting there they
return home to a hero's welcome. The president himself bestows a
medal, and doctors examining Peter find that the shock of the fall into
the ocean has restored his growth gland, so that after several years Peter
will reach a normal size. The news gladdens the family, but Peter is
thoughtful: although it will mean a normal life, there will be no more
flights with a seagull. The conclusion is a poignant one.

The jacket for the first edition of *The Fabulous Flight* advertised the
book as the reverse of Jonathan Swift's "fable" of Gulliver and the Lil-
liputians, but it is so only in the most superficial sense, in that Peter is
tiny in a world of what are, to him, giants. There is the delight of the
contrast of the small to the large that fills this novel, but Lawson is also
focusing on the contrast in size—conceived physically and metaphori-
cally—between childhood and adulthood. Here is the old story of the
small and, presumably, weak defeating the large and strong. Here, in
fact, diminuitive size is actually the very thing that will give Peter his
advantage. He can do what no one else in the world can do.

But Lawson is also describing the situation of all children, although
he would never be as explicit in doing this as, say, Maurice Sendak. In a
world where children are playing to the Gullivers, there is the desire to
see a reversal of roles, to fly freely, to save the day, to control the world
all around. And *control* is exactly the right word here. Although so very
small, Peter is absolutely self-contained; he is never bothered or made
anxious by his situation. The illustration of him being examined by a
doctor who is trying to solve the riddle of his shrinking size shows a

bemused young boy; it is the doctor who is confounded. Similarly, the quest is never hurried, never frenzied; Peter is able to deal with his situations himself; he is the child in charge of his own life. He is the daydream made into an adventure, the child whose very childishness gives him power.

In his merger of realism and fantasy, Lawson here tilts the balance quite heavily toward fantasy, with little that can be considered realism. In this merger, however—or perhaps along the interstices of this merger—Lawson establishes his exploration of friendship, which is at the very heart of this novel. As Peter grows smaller, so his friends grow fewer, until eventually his parents are forced to take him out of school, as he is no longer like others. His response is to find others like him, and in this he is successful: he meets Buck, the rabbit, as well as the mice and birds that form his army and air force corps. But most especially he meets Gus.

The friendship that Lawson develops between the boy and the seagull is crucial to the completion of the narrative and also what first strikes the reader. Gus and Peter are of like interests; they have almost the same responses at the same time. They both dislike London and Venice; they both feel that the Roman buildings are in disrepair; they both come to the conclusion that they should destroy the explosive. There is never any debate between them; there is immediate and instinctive agreement.

And there is also trust. Peter never doubts Gus's abilities as they begin the long hop. He is frightened by the squall they fly through but never threatened. He is sure of Gus's faithfulness while he stays in the scientist's castle. And he is confident that should he fall, Gus will be there to retrieve him—a confidence that is tested successfully when the shock waves do indeed toss them both into the ocean. The concluding poignancy of the novel comes about not only because their adventures are over, but because their relationship can never be the same once Peter starts to grow, once Peter moves back into the normal human world and leaves the fantasy world that had become so important to him, and of which Gus is a part.

Lawson's merger of fantasy and reality is not universally successful in *The Fabulous Flight*. The union of tour with quest is a union of the realistic with the fantastic, but the two often seem unequally yoked. Characters on a quest to save the world seem ill-situated to tour the Jersey coast along the way, or to frolic on Nantucket, or to view the changing of the guard at Windsor Castle. Similarly, once the quest is complete, it seems more likely that Gus and Peter would return immediately to one of the embassies; instead, they tour Italy and the Mediterranean. Meanwhile the family waits anxiously back home to hear if they are even alive. Unless Lawson wants to paint Peter as insensitive and even uncaring about his family, this seems an odd way to plot the novel.

The touring motif provides Lawson the opportunity to do what he does in *McWhinney's Jaunt:* illustrate great architectural sites. In *McWhinney's Jaunt* these would be American sites, both man-made and natural; in *The Fabulous Flight* Lawson begins with American sites but then proceeds to Europe, and in fact the illustrations of those European sites are among Lawson's finest of this type. The cover boasts a full-color illustration of Peter and Gus flying above Trafalgar Square. Interior black-and-white illustrations include those of Windsor Castle, the Arc de Triomphe, Venice, the Colosseum, and the well-known Notre Dame gargoyle who sticks his tongue out at Paris, the latter a drawing with which Lawson was particularly pleased.[4]

The quest motif gives the advantage of structure. Peter and Gus are on a mission, and all of the novel's episodes refer to this sense of mission. The movement from America to London to Copenhagen to Paris to Zargonia—a movement that is detailed in the map adorning the endpages—provides a structure missing from the other whimsical books, which often seem to meander. And it is the quest that allows for the development of the relationship between Gus and Peter and that perhaps accounts for the success of Lawson's depiction of their friendship.

The pivotal moment of the quest is not the successful retrieval of the explosive but the decision to destroy it so that no government might use it. Gus and Peter instinctively agree on this necessity, although Lawson prepares for it early in the novel by undercutting the seriousness of governments. When Gus and Peter experimentally land on the Capitol, they are blown off: "Gas, that's what. Hot air and gas. Why them ventilators come right out of the Senit Chamber" (44), explains Gus. Later, when Peter proposes his plan to his father, Lawson explains why Mr. Pepperell was so unusual in the government: "He had an imagination and an open mind" (49). Other figures are shown as silly and childish, including the two Supreme Court justices who squabble over the model trains.

Of Lawson's five books of this genre, perhaps it is the ending of *The Fabulous Flight* that makes it so much more satisfying and successful than the others. Any fantastic epic adventure must end with a changed protagonist and a changed world: one cannot go off fighting dragons and return to the same old stuff. But the epic adventure must also end

FROM ROBERT LAWSON, *THE FABULOUS FLIGHT* (BOSTON: LITTLE BROWN, 1949). REPRINTED BY PERMISSION OF MARTIN BRIGHT AND THE NINA F. BOWMAN ESTATE.

with home. The poignancy is generated by the mix of these elements—change and changelessness.

Smeller Martin

Smeller Martin (1950) uses a child protagonist who is given an extraordinary quality, but the novel's very emphasis on the young protagonist stands at the center of its difficulties—as well as its strengths. On the one hand the novel is the most diffuse of all Lawson's fantasies, and perhaps the least satisfying structurally. Although it begins with a focus on young Davey Martin's extraordinary quality, it quickly bleeds off into a series of plots and subplots that are only tangentially connected to this quality. On the other hand, however, the novel is stronger than any of the other four whimsical fantasies in its presentation of fully developed characters.

The result is a rather confused and disappointing book, not so much for what it is as for what it came close to being. The novel would have been stronger if Lawson had abandoned the fantasy elements and developed the very real and very human conflicts that the plot lines suggest. Because only several of the plot lines are connected by the fantasy element—and then only tangentially—Lawson might easily have dropped the fantastical altogether and focused instead on the moral choices that the characters make. And they are powerful moral choices—ones that, in a slightly different form, might make a reader shudder. In this form, they pass by almost with the shrug of a shoulder.

Young Davey Martin always knew that he had a powerful sense of smell, but he had not considered this at all extraordinary until his roommate at his Connecticut boarding school sensed the possibilities. Davey could, simply through smell, tell not only what was cooking for dinner but what other classmates had been doing all day: exploring in the woods, playing catch (he can tell by the smell that the boy had been using a catcher's mitt), experimenting about in a lab. His roommate, Skinny, collects bets on Davey's skill, and soon Davey becomes known at school as "Smeller."[5]

Back home at Lavender Hill for the summer, Davey lives with Rose the cook, McKinley the gardener, and his watchful Aunt Agatha. They form a loving and complete household. Davey's father is one of the country's most successful playwrights, his mother one of the country's most beloved actresses. The result is that they are rarely at home; they have bought Lavender Hill to provide some degree of normalcy in Davey's life, some kind of permanent place. But they are not a part of it, and in fact never appear in the novel; however, they do send presents, and on arriving home for the summer Davey finds a beautiful set of fieldglasses. McKinley has received a leather wallet, inscribed with initials, Rose a silk scarf, and Agatha her eighth wristwatch.

The cast of characters widens to include the Carter tribe—a jovial but naive grandfather who has run the family fortunes into the ground, a mad uncle, and Sonny Boy, once a friend of Davey but now a sophisticated 15 and unwilling to associate with a 12-year-old. There is also the Reverend Beasley, whose frequent tea visits are part of his pursuit of Aunt Agatha; Professor Benton, a retired Latin teacher with an interest in roses and antique guns; and Lieutenant Corrigan of the State Police, a man oppressed by the meanness of his job. These characters are all bound together both by geography—most of the events occur on Lavender Hill and the professor's neighboring home—and by Davey's sense of smell.

When the Carters come to cut hay, Davey shows Sonny Boy his field-glasses and tells him about McKinley's leather wallet. That evening, when Davey goes to find the glasses after helping the Carters pitch hay, they are gone. The next day his suspicions are confirmed when he smells the leather strap on Sonny Boy's shirt, but he is too troubled by his former friend's deception to confront him. Soon, however, McKinley finds that his wallet has also disappeared, and although Aunt Agatha sends to town for one just like it, the theft hangs heavy in the air. Again, Davey is sure that Sonny Boy took the wallet but is unwilling to confront him.

Aunt Agatha suggests that they both go to town for several days not just to shop but because she "felt that a short change would do them both good and help erase the memory of the recent unpleasant happenings, happenings so foreign to the usual quiet peace of Lavender Hill" (64). There they meet Professor Benton, who has just been to see the new movie starring Davey's mother, a movie that Davey found embarrassing. He is pleasant and friendly and asks the right sort of questions about school, and Davey immediately takes to him. They agree to meet at the Metropolitan Museum of Art the next day while Aunt Agatha shops, and there Professor Benton introduces Davey to the world of guns and armor, stressing the masterful artistry of the pieces. His reaction is awe: "Davey was almost dizzy with this wealth of beautiful design and workmanship" (71). The director of the museum is equally taken by Davey, and gives him a gun that he had purchased but found not to be authentic. Professor Benton's reaction to this suggests his growing admiration—and even love—for Davey: " 'By George,' Professor Benton chuckled, 'that's the first time I ever saw old Bill give away anything in his life. It's wonderful, my boy, to be Garda Garrison's son. Of course there's something in being a nice, decent, well-mannered young guy too' " (74).

Once back to Lavender Hill, Davey begins frequent trips over to the professor's house, where he finds that the professor is the author of the

Latin text that has plagued him in school; in fact, Professor Benton has retired early not only because of the financial success of that text but because he realizes that he is loathed by so many schoolchildren who suffer through his exercises. But Davey laughingly overlooks this and becomes a kind of apprentice. Professor Benton teaches him how to restore the guns, to care for them by oiling and scraping, how to load and shoot. Davey begins to spend much of his summer there, and Professor Benton comes to know Aunt Agatha better. Soon he is a rival to the Reverend Beasley, and then more than a rival.

On one of his visits, Davey meets Lieutenant Corrigan, who has no lead in his latest case but a leather strap left behind by a thief. Davey, simply by smelling it, is able to identify the leash as a strap for a German shepherd, and as somehow associated with a bakery. That is all the lieutenant needs to solve the case; he does not tell Davey, however, that he has just solved a murder case. But when one of the professor's prize guns is stolen, Davey has a more difficult situation to deal with. He smells the scent of Sonny Boy in the room, and he is sure that he has stolen it. He lies to Corrigan to protect his old friend, then goes to the Carter farm to convince Sonny Boy to return the gun. When confronted, Sonny Boy beats him. Aunt Agatha is aghast and Rose efficient; McKinley swears vengeance, but Davey will not tell them what has happened. The next day, however, the gun is returned, and Professor Benton recognizes that the events must be related; Lieutenant Corrigan agrees.

When the new barn on the Carter place is set ablaze, Davey thinks that McKinley must have found out and taken his vengeance. It happens that Professor Benton, Reverend Beasley, and Davey are eating with Aunt Agatha when they see the fire, so they all rush over. McKinley, too, has stopped, and Sonny Boy, seeing him, accuses him of setting the blaze. A mob of Carters soon approaches him, and the illustration suggests the possibility of a lynching. But Professor Benton and the Reverend stand between McKinley and the mob until Lieutenant Corrigan arrives to take charge. The tension is diffused, however, when the mad Carter uncle brags that he has started the fire, a pillar of fire like the Lord's (the Reverend Beasley has been trying to convert him). The uncle also reveals that Sonny Boy has a cache of stolen goods, and when they are found, Sonny Boy is arrested; Davey gets his fieldglasses back, McKinley another wallet.

In the fall, Davey returns to school. Soon after he receives two telegrams, one from Aunt Agatha telling him that his parents will be home for Christmas and that Professor Benton has asked for her hand, and the other from Professor Benton telling Davey that they would like his permission to marry. Davey, elated, borrows the money to send the telegram but stops just long enough to smell out the window to find what supper will be.

The ending suggests a kind of circular structure to the novel; in the conclusion, Davey is back where he has been, and although there is no essential change in his character, he nonetheless has a new uncle. His sense of smell has been instrumental in solving mysteries, although in both cases the identity of the thief is easily fixed: Sonny Boy was on site both times. But the ending itself is inconclusive on at least two fronts. First, Davey has not been able to protect his old friend, who, after a short time at a corrective farm, disappears with his car, presumably heading for Hollywood. There is a sense of a dead end here; Lieutenant Corrigan imagines him dead one day in a gutter. There is a terrible poignancy to this, although Davey seems almost unaware of it, and even the narrator treats it in a cavalier fashion. But for the reader, this dismissal is hard to accept. When Davey first realizes that Sonny Boy has stolen the gun, a series of vivid pictures flashes through his mind: "He and Sonny Boy down in the swimming hole—Sonny had taught him to swim. He and Sonny Boy skating and Sonny Boy building a fire to warm their feet and roast potatoes. They were hunting woodchucks, and Sonny Boy generously offered him the first shot. . . . Older, stronger, more skilled in everything than Davey, always helping him, always teaching him. . . . Then he saw Sonny Boy under the glaring lights at the police Barracks, surrounded by cops" (120). Not only do they share this past, but Sonny Boy and Davey do have another important connection: neither has parents that are at all present in his life. Davey's moral dilemma is a difficult one: he decides to lie in order to protect his friend. But once Sonny Boy is found out and arrested, he seems utterly and completely removed from Davey's life, and there is no sense that Davey mourns this. When Aunt Agatha notes that Sonny Boy has been shaped by his "early environment and education, and lack of opportunity" (148), Lieutenant Corrigan dismisses this, claiming that he is "rotten" and "all I know is what really goes on" (148). And so Sonny Boy disappears from the novel, but the meaning and significance of that disappearance is never explored, neither by Davey nor by the narrator.

The story of Lieutenant Corrigan seems to have more resolution, but it, too, is really only an unresolved dead end. After Sonny Boy is arrested, the lieutenant comes back to Lavender Hill to "blow off steam." Professor Benton's reaction to Corrigan is telling: "He's due to retire soon. . . . I hope he does; this thing is getting him down" (149). "This thing" is more than his job; it is the dreadful spectacle of stupid (his word), needless evil. It is the spectacle of Sonny Boy, or of that murderer, who, abandoned by his wife, had hoped to make one big impressive score to win her back and fumbled. The issue Lawson touches on here is a dark and complex one: How is one to respond to the evil in the world? But neither the lieutenant nor the narrator seriously grapples with that issue. Instead, Corrigan retires to raise great danes. The troubling suggestion is that one grapples with the issue simply by retiring from it.

But perhaps the most disturbing element of the novel is the role of Davey's parents. They are one of the most admired and loved couples in America; the mention of their name ensures instant recognition and special treatment. Stores open up on Sundays especially for them, and hotels make available their best rooms. Davey's life is one of comfortable privilege, lived on the edge of the frenetic pace of global parents whose life in the theater is more real, vivid, and central to them than their life at Lavender Hill. When they do come home (Davey can count on his fingers the number of times they have been there), they carry with them their frenzy: "These visits were always wonderful and exciting. There were always fabulous presents, brought to him from New York or London or Paris. There were guests coming and going, packages and telegrams arriving, the telephone ringing incessantly. . . . Both Mother and Father would relax and say how marvelously peaceful it was to be living in the country again. 'By George,' his father always said, 'this is really living. We must settle down soon, Garda, and get some pleasure out of life. This squirrel-cage existence we carry on is preposterous. Just as soon as the next play is settled . . . ' Mother would smile her wonderful smile and agree with him" (24). What is distinctly left out from this description is Davey; there is no sense that he is part of their lives even when they are at Lavender Hill. In fact, these visits never last more than a few days, and they end with tears, hasty packing, and quick farewells.

The quiet is in fact the state of normalcy. The narrator is never overtly critical of those parents, but clearly they are a very small part of Davey's life. Children's literature is, at its very core, about a search for home and family, and clearly Davey's position in *Smeller Martin* is one of a child in need of a family. Certainly his parents have provided for all his physical concerns, but their care ends with that provision, although there are at least some good intentions on their part: "When Davey was born his mother had insisted that they buy this country place. 'Davey is going to have a normal life,' she had said firmly. "He's not going to be dragged around from pillar to post like most theater children, and he's not going to be shunted off on schools and camps and governesses. Besides, when we can settle down this will be a real place to settle.' When it soon became apparent that they never would settle down, Father's sister Agatha came to take over, and remained" (28). Their good intentions dissipate quickly, for they cannot give up the life that pleases them, and it is a life that has no room for Davey. He is shunted off to boarding schools, and he does in fact end up with something like a governess.

The great difficulty of this novel, however—and perhaps it lies with the inappropriateness of the genre for these questions—is that the narrator never explores Davey's reaction to this neglect. Nor are his parents called to any kind of recount. There are some hints of the effect of the neglect in their relationship. When the fieldglasses are lost, Davey reacts to the act of the theft, not to the loss of a gift from his parents. Although others use the connection, Davey never introduces himself as someone connected to the famous actress. In fact, when others, even Professor Benton, seem to swoon over her, Davey never responds. The one time he does see her in a film in this novel, he is critical. Although everyone else in the audience raves, "Davey thought that with all the make-up on she didn't look nearly so beautiful as at home, and her acting seemed, to him, just plain silly. It made him feel quite embarrassed" (64). He imagines his mother in real life; the difficulty lies in the fact that for her, the movies are real life. But Davey will never go so far as to be angry with his parents for this disparity. And it seems that all is forgiven as long as there is the occasional visit—although again, Davey does not react to the news that his parents will be coming home for Christmas at the end of the novel—news that comes from Aunt Agatha rather than from them.

The refusal of the novel to deal fully with this issue might be defended, however, by its provision of an alternate family for Davey. When Agatha comes to live at Lavender Hill, she becomes a real, permanent part of the household; in fact, she is identified with the name of the house: Davey is always able to tell where she is because she wears a lavender scent. She clearly comes to love Davey and becomes "more of a mother to Davey, really, than his own mother" (25). Professor Benton is Davey's father figure. He quickly comes to like Davey for his decency but then is able to speak with him not as a professor or as a mere neighbor but as a friend; he is able to ask the "right sort" of questions about school. He enjoys Davey's visits and teaches him a craft that he loves, sharing with Davey the things that matter most to him. They spend long summer hours together as Davey is taught to refurbish guns and then to shoot them. After Davey is beaten and the professor figures out why, he begins to recognize how closely he is attached to his family: "I would be tremendously proud to have him as a—nephew" (132). The hesitation before "nephew" works two ways. First, he might just as easily have said "son," as he is quickly taking on a father's duties and coming to love Davey. Second, he is announcing his very real love for Aunt Agatha, and her response is an almost giddy happiness.

About this relationship Davey is clear. At the conclusion of the novel they both seek his permission to marry, a strong signal that he is a crucial part of their world. They also look for his "enthusiastic" blessing and plan to marry during his holidays. Professor Benton's letter stresses not only the upcoming marriage but his new relationship to Davey: in noting that Aunt Agatha's acceptance is conditional on Davey's blessing, he writes, "I shall not attempt to influence you in any manner. You have seen enough of me and my ways to form your own opinion as to whether or not I would make a possible uncle" (155). Davey's response is "enthusiastic," for he recognizes that Professor Benton and Aunt Agatha will be much more than aunt and uncle to him.

But they are not the only members of Davey's family. There is also Rose, the cook, whose matronly and fussy love is expressed through her food and cleaning. And there is McKinley, the gardner and butler, who essentially plays the role of the older brother. He does not teach Davey as much as share his enthusiasms: the love of outdoor work, the excitement of a good blaze, the stealth of the hunt. He is what Sonny Boy is no longer: the companion in adventure. If his childlike simplicity is seen as degradation by current standards, it was not so seen by Lawson, who allows McKinley to play a crucial role in Davey's life. He is the friend to a boy who has no other summer friends, and for Davey, he is enough.

The issues the novel presents, then, are often dark ones: the divided family and neglectful parents; the nature versus nurture question, focusing on how one is led to good or evil; the genesis of a lynching; the possibility of reformation; the terrible realization of blighted hopes. And yet the novel maintains a consistently light, almost comic tone—one appropriate to a whimsical fantasy but not appropriate to those darker issues. Still, to find these issues raised at all in a children's novel of 1950 is somewhat remarkable. This was the time of the secure island worlds of Robert McCloskey's vision, not the isolated child of Maurice Sendak's work. If the presentation of the broken family is today the impetus behind many a plot sequence in children's novels, it was most uncommon when Lawson conceived of *Smeller Martin,* and it gives this novel a significance that it might not otherwise have.

McWhinney's Jaunt

Of all of Lawson's protagonists, Professor McWhinney may perhaps be the least likable. There is a certain arrogance about him—the result of his profession, no doubt. There is a concern for money, a lust for Hollywood that seems small, and a condescending attitude toward his wife, whom he leaves to her sewing because he finds her boring. In fact, it turns out that the entire short tale is a gimmick, a come-on to an unsuspecting listener who must hear about the long voyage of McWhinney (led, perhaps, by his "glittering eye") before he discovers that McWhinney is actually trying to sell him some Z-Gas—a bargain the customer agrees to but McWhinney never keeps.

McWhinney's Jaunt (1951) has the nonsense and exaggerated quality that the tales of the person to whom it is dedicated—Baron von Munchhausen—have. The illustration accompanying the title page announces these qualities: a bespectacled fellow wearing a battered stovepipe hat looks out at the reader, framed, as with a halo, by the mundane circlet of a bicycle tire—and even this is battered and one of its spokes bent. His smile suggests a kind of innocence, and although the book does not completely bear this out, this is in some measure the story of an innocent. He heads west to Hollywood where he hopes for fame, fortune, and the girl. He gets none of these.

Beneath this story line, however, lies another subtle search. While Professor McWhinney yearns for glamour, he misses the extraordinary world that lies just below him. McWhinney might be focusing on the practical aspects of securing his empty dream, but Lawson dwells instead on what the man misses: the landscape of America. The reader, particularly through the illustrations, sees what the narrator continues to miss, even after he has discovered the meaninglessness of his own dream. McWhinney is Lawson's depiction of the eager and frenetic American tourist.

The book opens with the appearance of Professor McWhinney in the driveway of Mr. Purslane, who "was sitting in his garden resting."[6] (He, too, has missed the significance of the landscape that lies outside of his garden.) Professor McWhinney rides up his driveway, his bicycle a few feet off the ground, and begins to tell him of his discovery of Z-Gas, a gas that gives buoyancy to his bicycle tires so that he can ride through the air.

After selling some of the gas for $50, Professor McWhinney heads west, crossing the Hudson River by bicycling up the supporting cables of the George Washington Bridge. He has a series of nonsense adventures—his tires expand over the steel mills of Pennsylvania, roadside cabins are torn apart by his bicycle lifting through their ceilings, and he wins a bicycle race in a small Missouri town. But he always seems to be missing the significance of what he passes. "I found Missouri as tiresome as Ohio, Indiana and Illinois, being also mostly corn" (30), he complains. In Oklahoma he uses an umbrella to protect himself from oil geysers; in the southwest he camps under the stars; and at the Grand Canyon he earns a thousand dollars by apparently bicycling over the canyon on some kite string.

When he finally reaches Hollywood, he finds that fame and fortune are not to be his. He demonstrates his astonishing discovery to several movie producers, only to find that art can do whatever his discovery can do: " 'There's nothing there that we couldn't do with mirrors and a couple of wires,' Mr. McPhysh said. 'Sorry, Professor.' He turned on his heel and walked to his waiting car" (58). When McWhinney leaves for Las Vegas, he is disappointed again. His flying bicycle startles the cattle on a set on which Gloria Glamora is working. He rescues her but finds that she is an unattractive shrew: "I therefore departed, my last Hollywood illusion completely laid in the dust" (64).

It is this sense of illusion that he must overcome, but in fact he seems unable to do so. He returns over the Boulder Dam and the Rocky Mountains. But during his stay in Yellowstone Park, his bicycle is damaged by a bear and most of the gas leaks out of the back tire. He moves some from the front tire to the back, but now his bicycle can only rise a few feet into the air. He returns home with depleted resources, stopping to tell his story to those he meets, hoping that they will buy some Z-Gas, which he promises to send once he has arrived home. It seems, however, that he forgets his promise, for the patient Mr. Purslane is still waiting.

Over and again Professor McWhinney misses the reality while he is in search of illusion. In fact, it would not be difficult to read this story as

Lawson's parable, a warning against looking too much to Hollywood, with its fancy and false glitz and illusion, and ignoring the grandeur that marks America. When Professor McWhinney leaves Hollywood, bitterly disappointed, he heads to Boulder Dam, but he misses its significance. He finds it impressive but goes on to find his own performance even more engaging:

> I rode across the dam several times which, of course, was no unusual feat; thousands of motorists have done it. I did, however, make my performance somewhat different by suddenly turning, when halfway across, and riding up the entire length of Lake Mead, a rather beautiful body of water.
> This caused no little excitement among the tourists atop the dam. (66)

The focus here is on his bicycling and the reaction of the tourists; it is not on the grandeur of the dam, although there is an aside thrown to the beauty of the lake. The illustration that accompanies this page, however, suggests a different perspective. A view from above the dam spreads it out in all its majesty, the valley heading off the page and into the distance. Although the professor is smiling as he rides above the lake (perhaps a self-satisfied smile rather than one of awe), no one is looking at him; despite his claim, there is no apparent excitement among the tourists.

The same difficulty accompanies him to Yellowstone Park. "The scenery, the geyser, and the steaming pools were most interesting and these beautiful hot water pools gave me and opportunity to do some much needed laundry work" (70), he informs Mr. Purslane. But the beginning of this compound sentence seems belied by the ending. Yellowstone seems memorable not for its scenery, for which he gives no details at all, but instead for its usefulness as a laundry. Certainly there is the element of the American tall tale here—using a geyser to wash clothes—but there remains beneath this tall tale the sense that something very important has been missed—something distinctly American.

All of what the professor sees seems insignificant in the face of Hollywood. When he is asked to stay at the Grand Canyon, he tells the manager who invites him that his mind was "set on Hollywood and higher things" (52), an odd union and one never explained. If he ranks Hollywood as among the higher things, then he must have been truly disappointed when he finds that Hollywood is sham and mirrors; even Gloria Glamora is not what she appeared to be on the screen.

FROM ROBERT LAWSON, *MCWHINNEY'S JAUNT* (BOSTON: LITTLE, BROWN, 1951). REPRINTED BY PERMISSION OF MARTIN BRIGHT AND THE NINA F. BOWMAN ESTATE.

What is poignant about McWhinney's jaunt is that he learns nothing. Having discovered the hollowness of Hollywood, he is unable to find anything else of significance. He continues to miss what lies around him during his trip home. His goal has now changed; he wishes to return to what he has previously described as a rather dreary classroom. Meanwhile, he soars with ospreys, finding them useful but not particularly beautiful or inspiring. (In the illustration for this scene, the osprey looks out at the reader as if to suggest that it, at least, finds something remarkable in all of this.)

Few tall tales end with such a disappointing whine as this one does: "It is probable that the Professor has been too busy with his new classes to get around to it (i.e. sending a vial of Z-Gas to Mr. Purslane). It is also just possible that, being somewhat absent-minded, he has forgotten all about it" (77). For this is indeed a tall tale, in which astonishing adventures (flying above the landscape) are recounted in the most unastonished voice. The same narrative strategy is frequently used in the telling of Paul Bunyan, Pecos Bill, and Davy Crockett stories, but here the narrative voice is primarily the professor's, and instead of creating humor through undercutting the enormity of the adventures, this voice degenerates into a sales pitch. If the point of this short parable is to be sensed, then the reader must get beyond the intrusive narration of Professor McWhinney.

McWhinney's Jaunt began with a tall tale conception but faltered with a poorly chosen narrative strategy and an even more poorly conceived narrator. Baron von Munchhausen would not have been pleased with the result.

Chapter Six
The Collaborative Works

In 1939, T. H. White's *The Sword in the Stone* was published, the text accompanied by a goodly number of White's own simple line drawings. The endpapers, however, were the work of Robert Lawson, and this illustration is anything but simple. Filled with the characters and events of the novel, the illustration is a collection, almost a collage, of narrative images. It is a world of action; nothing seems in stasis except the sleepy owl on Merlin's shoulder, connected to Merlin's hat with a spun web. Hawks and owls fly across the sky, their talons extended. Dogs set upon a boar, a hunter takes aim at the unsuspecting Questing Beast as an unseen giant approaches him with drawn sword. In the distance, knights joust. All is at war.

In the center foreground, however, Wart, a hawk on his wrist, is instructed by the comically fierce Merlin. Wart seems to observe the uproar around him, the disharmony that breeds the murderous activity of talons and swords and lances. Beside him, in one of the few uncrowded spaces of the illustration, the sword stands in the stone, glowing, suggesting that it, used properly, might control some of what is occurring in the landscape around it. But Wart has not yet reached for it; he is still learning.

Lawson had been illustrating books for nine years before he came to this task; this same year would see the publication of *Ben and Me,* the first book that he had both written and illustrated. This illustration for *The Sword in the Stone* comes at a pivotal point in the illustrating career he had enjoyed. In it, he found his greatest strength: narrative illustration. Essentially, this one two-page spread tells the entire story of *The Sword in the Stone*: here is the young observant Wart, the dismal world around him filled with violence and aggression, and the sword, waiting for the true king to draw it and restore some kind of order. Here is art as story, where the illustrations play a narrative role rather than a decorative one. In fact, the story is told as much by the illustrations as by the text.

Lawson began his career as a children's book illustrator with three fantasies by Arthur Mason, a now-forgotten novelist. *The Wee Men of*

FROM T. H. WHITE, *THE SWORD IN THE STONE*
(NEW YORK: G. P. PUTNAM'S SONS, 1939).

Ballywooden (1930), *From the Horn of the Moon* (1931), and *The Roving Lobster* (1931) are all fantasies that seem to mean much more than they do, and are more derivative than they ought to be. The first two are set in Ireland, and Lawson plays with Irish motifs in his illustrations, particularly in terms of dress. *The Wee Men of Ballywooden* is about Danny O'Fay and the leprechaun-like men who repay his kindnesses with fish. It is a long text, with only four full-page illustrations, each of which is a literal representation of the text—with one exception. When the Wee Men approach a lagooned island, Mason gives no description other than the fact that coconut trees grow there; Lawson endows the island with oversized, fantastical trees and jumping fish. It is an illustration closer to Louis Glanzman's work for Astrid Lindgren's Pippi Longstocking books than to Lawson's later illustrations. *The Roving Lobster* is set on some anonymous coast, where a lobster leaves his life in the sea because he feels that the stars are peering at him. He encounters seagulls, owls, goats, and an instrumental crane, and he finally returns to the sea in a visionary moment. The pen-and-ink illustrations are hard to differentiate from those of many illustrators working at mid-century. There are,

FROM ARTHUR MASON, *THE WEE MEN OF BALLYWOODEN* (GARDEN CITY, N.Y.: DOUBLEDAY, DORAN, 1930; NEW YORK: VIKING PRESS, 1952). REPRINTED BY PERMISSION OF MARTIN BRIGHT AND THE NINA F. BOWMAN ESTATE.

however, flashes of the humor that would mark Lawson's later work. In one illustration the lobster shoves a great claw out of a bubble blanket that he had built around himself, and Lawson adds the detail of a tasseled nightcap to stress the comedy.

The first real hint of Lawson's skills in children's literature comes with Margery Williams Bianco's *The Hurdy-Gurdy Man* (1933), the story of a musician who comes to a perfectly neat, perfectly tidy little town where no one seems to need any music. When the hurdy-gurdy man starts to play in the town square, however, all the children rush to him; they refuse to listen to the teacher or the mayor, and as the music gets faster and faster all the adults are finally drawn in, until the whole town is dancing to the tunes of the hurdy-gurdy man. Lawson's settings are as detailed and as full as he would later use in his historical novels, but this is his first book to combine illustration with text to create a meaningful whole. To illustrate the line "Every child in town, by now, was gathered around the hurdy-gurdy,"[1] Lawson depicts the teacher, standing with her arms outstretched in front of her school. The children are in a crowd way off in the distance, separated from their teacher by a large area of white space. In fact, Lawson uses a great deal of white space in this book, suggesting the emptiness of the town. The last illustration is full and disordered, suggesting that while the town is no longer perfectly ordered, it is a happier place.

Most of the early novels Lawson illustrated have today been forgotten; a work like Ella Young's *The Unicorn with Silver Shoes* (1932) is certainly not remembered, and Lawson's illustrations do little to give it life. Most of the illustrations are stiff and literal interpretations of a single sentence. The same is true for Barbara Ring's *Peik* (1932), a Norwegian novel about a young orphan's education in life. There are, however, moments in *Peik* when Lawson's narrative abilities are suggested: in an illustration that depicts Piet's guardian about to shave, Piet wakes up and cries, "You might cut yourself."[2] Lawson uses shock on both of their faces to show a mutual surprise, but he also includes a solid white space to separate them and suggest their strangeness with each other. Later, after they have grown close, Lawson depicts the Professor, as he is called, carrying Piet to bed. The Professor's grasp is loving, and Piet has his arm thrown around his neck. The Professor's content, pleased expression suggests how close he has become to Piet.

Lawson's 1935 illustrations for Elizabeth Coatsworth's *The Golden Horseshoe* use a larger format, but again work decoratively. This historical novel set in the early days of colonial America includes illustrations that

FROM MARGERY WILLIAMS BIANCO, *THE HURDY-GURDY MAN*
(NEW YORK: OXFORD UNIVERSITY PRESS, 1933).

function as set pieces; they do not intend to convey narrative information. At one point in the narrative, a chief Opechancanough comes to
bring a gift to the royal governor. Ten years later Lawson would have
drafted an illustration that focused on characters' reactions to this
event—perhaps focusing on the governor's shocked or moved or pleased
reaction. But in this text Lawson illustrates the eight men carrying a lit-
ter as a stately tableau.

These same patterns continued until the late 1930s; in fact, for some
time, Lawson was not to illustrate a book that was truly appropriate to his
vision, particularly his comic vision. He illustrated a number of historical
novels, including John Marquand's *Haven's End* (1933), about a small
New England seacoast town; Helen Dixon Bates's *Betsy Ross* (1936) and

Francis Scott Key (1936), fictionalized biographical accounts; Emma Gilders Sterne's *Drums of Monmouth* (1935), set in colonial America, and *Miranda Is a Princess* (1937), set in medieval Spain; Elizabeth Gales's *Seven Beads of Wampum* (1936), with half of its illustrations done in silhouettes; Clarence Stratton's *Swords and Statues* (1937), set in sixteenth-century Italy; Jean Rosmer's *In Secret Service* (1937), set during the Napoleonic wars; and Maribelle Cormack's *Wind of the Vikings* (1937), set in the Orkney islands.

In these novels Lawson's illustrations are strong in their depiction of landscapes and particularly city scenes; the architectural details are both accurate and engaging. The figures, however, remain stilted and lifeless, as if they are posing rather than truly acting and moving. The frontispiece for *In Secret Service,* for example, seems to put its characters stiffly on a stage. This stagey feel occurs as well in Lawson's illustrations for Walter Russell Bowie's *The Story of Jesus* (1937), where the depiction of Joseph telling stories to the young Jesus is detailed and even narratorial in its use of the Roman soldiers but is stiff in its depiction of character, particularly Joseph. It is perhaps telling that in *Drums of Monmouth;* William Haines's *Slim* (1934), with only seven Lawson illustrations spread over 400 pages; and Eleanor Farjeon's *One Foot in Fairyland* (1938) the illustrations are in fact called "decorations."

In 1937 Lawson illustrated several poetry collections; they were to point the direction of his future work. John E. Brewton's *Under the Tent of the Sky* (1937) is a verse collection about animals, and Lawson's work here is humorless and literal only. A small holstein decorates the foreword, a turkey the table of contents, a calf the introductory page. The illustrations—and there are not many—are truly decorative only. But in Ruth A. Barnes's *I Hear America Singing* (1937), a folk poetry collection, Lawson's illustrative vision begins to expand. He is on his favorite turf here: the story of America. And he is experimenting some, in that for the first time he is using two tones in his illustration, incorporating a burnt orange. Again, many of the illustrations are merely decorative. At the beginning of each section of the poems, however, Lawson includes a full-page illustration that, while it smacks of the tableau, also begins to include the narrative art that would mark his later work. The illustration depicting a canal boat being pulled through the water also includes passengers who have come on the rooftop to watch a storm coming in over the fields. Another shows a cowboy taming a horse; the horse bucks so high it pushes the cowboy out of the illustration's frame.

Perhaps the most effective illustration is that preceding the grouping of poems on homesteading: a young boy looks down from a hilltop over

FROM JEAN ROSMER, *IN SECRET SERVICE,* TRANS. VIRGINIA OLCOTT
(PHILADELPHIA: J. B. LIPPINCOTT, 1937).

his family's sod house. The view is spectacular: hills fold into one another far away into the horizon, and a huge cloud billows up like a mountain in the sky. It seems as though there should be a sense of peace and plentitude, but there is not. The boy stands with a hoe in his hand, a hoe much too big for him. Dressed in raggedy clothes and exhausted, he looks out not only at beauty but at a task so daunting as to sap his courage: How with one hoe can he create a farm from an unforgiving land? The many-layered emotions depicted in this illustration mark it as one of Lawson's most successful to date.

Lawson also used two tones in Helen Dean Fish's *Four and Twenty Blackbirds* (1937), a collection of 24 nursery rhymes. Here again Lawson excels in his landscape scenes; the first, to illustrate "Little Dame Crump," depicts a miller's cottage by a stream; the water is straddled by a stone bridge. The trees, the ordered fields, the gently sloped hills, the lush grass growing down to water's edge—all suggest a peaceful, once-upon-a-time setting. The illustrations for *Four and Twenty Blackbirds* are in general much stronger in terms of their narrative quality—a quality encouraged by the subject matter. Many of the characters are animals, and Lawson not only dresses them in human clothes but endows them with human qualities of expression and movement: the cat dressed up as a mock-robber, the dog dressed as a doctor, the "comical cat" loading a musket. And here, more than in any of the other collections, Lawson uses his illustrations to extend text. In "Old Crummles," for example, Crummles rises from his grave to marry a woman picking apples from the tree above him; the tone is light and mock-horrific, but Lawson extends that by depicting the woman as a set of grotesque contrasts: her dress, her stride, her hairstyle—everything suggests that she is young, one ready to become a wife. But her face shows her an old crone—appropriate for one about to marry a corpse. In "Joe Dobson," the old story of the husband and wife who exchange tasks to see who performs more household work, Lawson gives over a full page to the distraught Joe, whose clothes are torn, whose leg is bloodied, and whose household is a wreck. Lawson's illustration depicts the carnage of his day in the house; he sits in the midst of it all, defeated, while his wife towers over him, a benign complaisance on her face.

This growth into narrative and extension of the text began to develop fully with Lawson's most important collaboration, that with Munro Leaf. It began in 1936 with Munro Leaf's short story, *The Story of Ferdinand*. The collaboration would extend to four books with *Wee Gillis* (1938), *Aesop's Fables* (1941), and *The Story of Simpson and Sampson* (1941).

Of these four, the second garnered a Caldecott Honor, and *The Story of Ferdinand* might have won the Caldecott Medal itself, but the award had not yet been established. With Leaf, Lawson began to seriously exercise the art of narrative illustration, using his pictures to extend the text by developing elaborate and pivotal settings, by delineating characterization, by focusing narrative action, and by establishing new and unexpected—and usually humorous—stances.

Much has been written of the apparent simplicity and complex meaning of *The Story of Ferdinand*.[3] This familiar story of the bull who would rather sniff the flowers than fight has been interpreted as a kind of pacifist manifesto, a story remembered more for its meaning than its action—if those two could be separated. But much of the success of this work comes from the interplay of text and illustration, as both work back and forth to complement and extend the other. The text is placed on the left-hand page, the illustrations on the right—a pattern broken on only the first and last pages. The text itself has the simple, straightforward diction of a fable, which is the effect for which Leaf is looking. But the illustrations elaborate that simplicity and establish not only much of the humor of the story but also its narrative progression. "Once upon a time in Spain,"[4] the first page reads, and Lawson illustrates the text with soaring, impossibly high towers that reach up into the clouds. Beneath them, gentle hills fold down into meadows where bulls and calves are grazing. But with the second page—"there was a little bull and his name was Ferdinand"—Lawson moves quickly from the grandiose to the particular, as he focuses on Ferdinand as a calf. It is this illustration of Ferdinand that first shows his interest in butterflies and especially flowers; this interest will not be mentioned in the text for three more pages.

In these two pages Lawson has not only established setting, suggested character, and anticipated the plot line but has also established the dichotomy between the proud world of humans and the safe, individually oriented world of the peaceful Ferdinand. The third illustration—this of the six calves with whom he lives—suggests another dichotomy. They are all active, butting herds, chasing a butterfly, looking angrily at a turtle. The fourth illustration turns from this active and aggressive world, as Lawson had turned from the grandiose Spanish landscape, to focus on Ferdinand, who is pictured diminutively, moving away from the reader. The short phrases that accompany these pages—"but not Ferdinand"—suggest not only how quickly the pages are to be turned by the child reader but how much the text depends on the illustration to convey meaning and contrast.

The remaining illustrations of Ferdinand as a calf work out the impli-cations of these two opening sets of contrasts. The next illustration sug-gests a span in time: "As the years went by Ferdinand grew and grew until he was very big and strong." The contrast between the calf and the muscular, thick-necked bull is a striking one, but here Lawson is at pains to show connections. Ferdinand's droopy eyelids and the flower that protrudes from his mouth suggest that little has changed in his charac-ter, just as the following illustration of his companion bulls shows that little has changed in their characters; two of them are bandaged, the result of their aggression. The first illustration of the adult Ferdinand is also foreboding, however. In growing "very big and strong," Ferdinand is now available for the bull fights; the vulture that watches him from a tree suggests the implications of this growth.

In the next few pages, Lawson alternates between setting Ferdinand off in the distance and moving him to the foreground. The illustrations using distance suggest how far away Ferdinand is from the men with funny hats who come to find fierce bulls; Ferdinand walks slowly and contentedly away from them. But immediately afterwards three succes-sive illustrations show various parts of Ferdinand as he is stung by a bee, moving from rear, to head, and then back to the rear, now mostly out of the picture, giving an almost cinematic feel to the three, as though a film editor has moved from event to reaction to aftermath.

That same distancing is used in the bullfighting scene itself. After a series of illustrations where Lawson undercuts the seriousness of events by picturing the banderilleros, picadores, and even the matadore comi-cally—a bluejay perches on one of the picadores' lances, and one of the banderilleros steps on the heel of another—Lawson pulls back to give a series of pictures showing the immense scale of the arena; Ferdinand is dwarfed and would be lost except for the fact that he is in a center of the arena. The diminutive Ferdinand is set against close-ups of the bull fighters, so that their fear of him is exaggerated and comic. The final illustration, in which Ferdinand is returned to his beloved cork tree, again suggests the utter peace of Ferdinand and his lack of desire to be at the center of action.

Lawson's illustrations, then, are integral to an understanding of *The Story of Ferdinand*. They comically undercut, they extend narrative, and in their distancing they support the essential meaning of the story. This is the first collaborative work in which Lawson had seamlessly united text and illustration, and the book marked his real development as a narrative artist and was a turning point in his career as an illustrator.

Lawson followed the page patterns of *The Story of Ferdinand* in *Wee Gillis* and *Simpson and Sampson:* each book opens with a scene that establishes the setting and then proceeds with the text on the left-hand page, the illustration on the right. The opening illustration of *Wee Gillis* is set at the foot of the mountains of Scotland, foreshadowing the central issues of the story: whether Wee Gillis will live as a highlander stalking stags or a lowlander herding cattle. *Simpson and Sampson* opens with a castle scene, the formal structures of the castle being undercut by homey details: laundry hanging from the turrets, ducks by the castle gate, a fellow fishing in the moat. Here, too, the opening scene establishes some of the concerns of the book, as formal and expected structures give way to human concerns.

Many of the same techniques that Lawson applied to *The Story of Ferdinand* are used in these tales as well. There is, for example, the same alternation between distanced images of Wee Gillis and images that place him in the foreground. At times, like Ferdinand, Wee Gillis is dwarfed by the surrounding landscape. At other times he is much closer, particularly when he begins to blow the bagpipes that signal his great gift; here Lawson shows only a profile. In *Simpson and Sampson,* Lawson uses this device for comic effect, as the reader moves from a full-scale illustration of the stately and elegant Lady Miranda, complete with long train, to the following image, which pictures Lady Miranda's head jerked back as Sampson steps on that train, with the ensuing wreckage to Lady Miranda's coiffure and composure. This sequence of illustrations depicting Lady Miranda suggests Lawson's continuing focus on narrative illustration. Here Lady Miranda moves from composure to wrath, although her pages remain impassive.

In fact, the illustrations for *Simpson and Sampson* convey, as in *The Story of Ferdinand,* most of the narrative information. Leaf writes that "even while they were tiny babies and had just been given their names, anyone could see that Simpson was very good and Sampson was very bad."[5] As in *The Story of Ferdinand,* it is left to the illustration to objectify what is abstract. In the accompanying illustration Lawson pictures a sleeping Simpson and a Sampson in the midst of a tantrum, rocking his cradle and smashing everything he can. Later, when Simpson is a knight, the narrator suggests that "whenever Simpson tried to right a wrong and be helpful to the peasants who lived around there, he would mess things up and they would be worse off that they were before he came." The accompanying illustration depicts Simpson having tramped with his horse through a just-sprouting vegetable garden, having smashed a cold frame, upset a bee hive, decimated a hedge, and scattered geese and cows.

In *Wee Gillis* the narrative element of the illustration is weaker, or perhaps it is better to say that the illustrations are directed less to the linear narrative and more to the larger meanings of the story. When Wee Gillis is shown against the backdrop of vast landscapes, his diminutive size suggests the enormity of the difficult choice before him. This is, in the end, a story about making choices, and each of the illustrations works toward that emphasis. When Gillis goes down to the lowlands, for example, the narrator suggests that "every day he rose early and ate a large bowl of oatmeal."[6] The illustration shows a huge bowl in front of Gillis, with a mug in front of him decorated with a cow; his hat hangs on a pair of cow horns. Later, when in the highlands, he has the same breakfast, and Lawson uses the same illustration, except that now the mug is decorated with a stag, and Wee Gillis's hat hangs on a pair of antlers.

Later illustrations put Gillis between his two uncles, each of whom urges Gillis to follow his own way of life. Gillis's face, as it is for much of the book, is impassive; he seems unable to be enthusiastic about either way of life. He smiles for the first time in the book only when he sees the set of bagpipes that no one else can play. Here for the first time is a choice that he can make based on his own interests—although his ability in that area has been shaped by his experience in the lowlands and the highlands: he has become able to play these enormous bagpipes because of the lung development made while calling for cows and holding his breath so as not to startle the stags.

All three Leaf books end similarly; like parables, they suggest meanings and conclude with contentment. Lawson uses his final illustration to suggest that contentment. In *The Story of Ferdinand,* he concludes with an illustration of Ferdinand under his cork tree, where, the narrator interposes, "he is very happy." In *Wee Gillis,* Gillis sits back on a chair, the enormous bagpipes under his arm; he is playing contentedly, partially for the four children who peer over the wall but mostly for himself, having found his true vocation. Now instead of having to choose one spot to live, "Wee Gillis is welcome down in the Lowlands and up in the Highlands, but most of the time he just stays in his house halfway up the side of a medium-sized hill." *Simpson and Sampson* ends with the twins grasping each other's hands, smiling and touching each other for the first time in the book: "When nobody cheered for either one of them Simpson and Sampson started to think, and they saw how silly the whole thing was and they got down off their horses, called off the fight, and had a wonderful party instead, and everybody there had a very good time." In each case, illustration complements and extends textual meaning.

FROM *WEE GILLIS* BY MUNRO LEAF, ILLUSTRATED BY ROBERT LAWSON.
COPYRIGHT 1938 BY MUNRO LEAF AND ROBERT LAWSON, RENEWED (C)
1996 BY MUNRO LEAF AND JOHN W. BOYD; EXECUTOR OF THE ESTATE
OF ROBERT LAWSON. USED BY PERMISSION OF VIKING PENGUIN, A DIVI-
SION OF PENGUIN BOOKS USA INC.

122

In 1941 Lawson and Leaf also collaborated on *Aesop's Fables,* the only work they did together for a press other than Viking. Forgotten today, the book is notable principally as a measure of how far Lawson's narrative art had come. Most of the fables are decorated with sepia-colored line drawings, all filled with energy and movement depicting the action of the fable. But Lawson also includes nine full-page illustrations, all framed, which not only depict but develop the action of the fable. For "The Horse and the Stag," in which the wild horse allies with man to defeat the stag, discovering only too late that now he is the slave of the man, Lawson pictures a stone-age fellow, holding a stone spear and with a gleeful expression. The horse's eyes pop out, like Ferdinand the bull's when he is stung, for the bit in his mouth shows his fate. Behind them both, the wild stag watches. For "The Wood and the Chopper," in which trees naively give wood to a woodsman so that he can make an ax handle, which he then uses to chop them down, Lawson shows ancient trees, their expressions full of anger and distress. The woodsman chops energetically at the base of an oak, his stance and handling of the axe is expert and full of movement—quite different from the stiff woodsman of *I Hear America Singing.*

It is perhaps not exaggeration to say that *The Story of Ferdinand* established Robert Lawson's reputation as an illustrator of children's books. In 1942, his editor at Little, Brown, Alfred McIntyre, decided to reprint Andrew Lang's *Prince Prigio;* his preface indicates something of how he viewed Lawson and suggests by its direction to children how Lawson was perceived by his readers: finding the book on his shelves, McIntyre "suddenly thought, Why isn't this just the book for Robert Lawson to illustrate? As perhaps you know, Mr. Lawson drew the pictures for *Ferdinand* and *Mr. Popper's Penguins* and *Poo-Poo and the Dragons,* as well as for . . . several stories of his own. So *Prince Prigio* was sent to Mr. Lawson and he read it and he liked it and he said he wanted to illustrate it."[7] Lawson is here identified by his collaborative work, beginning with *The Story of Ferdinand. Prince Prigio,* a pseudo-medieval tale about an unpopular prince, is appropriate to Lawson's comic vision in its merger of the serious with the humorous, its undercutting of pretension and expectation by a comic vision. *Poo-Poo and the Dragons* (1942), a contemporary fantasy by C. S. Forester, also uses the motif of the dragons, although comically undercut. In this text Lawson again tries to merge the serious with the comic, but the book is by a man skilled at writing romantic and adventurous sea novels, not children's stories, and the result is not memorable. In fact, *Prince Prigio* and *Poo-Poo and the Dragons* are today notable principally as books that suggest Lawson's standing as an illustrator.

The late 1930s and early 1940s were some of Lawson's most productive years. He illustrated four books in 1936, nine in 1937, and three in 1938, including *Mr. Popper's Penguins,* by Richard and Florence Atwater. The story is a familiar one: Mr. Popper, locked in as a painter in the sleepy town of Stillwater, yearns to explore one of the poles. When he sends a letter to Admiral Drake during his expedition to the South Pole, Drake is so impressed that he sends Mr. Popper a gift, a penguin, whom Mr. Popper names Captain Cook. It soon becomes an important part of the household, although it causes some difficulties with local authorities. Soon, however, it begins to pine, and Mr. Popper is delighted when a zookeeper sends him another penguin, Greta. Eventually there are 10 more penguins, and the Poppers' finances are hard-pressed until a showman recognizes the potential of a penguin act and the Poppers go on tour. When the tour is finished, Mr. Popper faces a difficult choice. A movie company has offered him a contract with the birds that will make Mr. Popper very rich, but Admiral Drake has returned and offered to take the penguins to the North Pole to start a colony there. Mr. Popper chooses the latter, and is overjoyed when Admiral Drake asks him to go along on the expedition, thus fulfilling his first and greatest dream.

Again using two tones, as he had in *I Hear America Singing* and *Four and Twenty Blackbirds,* Lawson crafted illustrations that captured not only the humor but the poignancy of the story. On the one hand this is a story of a man whose life is turned upside down by a flock of penguins; on the other, it is the story of a man who lives a shrunken life, whose dream seems an impossibility and who suddenly and unexpectedly finds that the dream will indeed be made reality. Lawson balances these two sides of the story in his illustrations. When Captain Cook arrives, for example, he literally jumps out of the crate that Mr. Popper has taken apart in his beautifully wallpapered parlor. Mr. Popper's expression is one of delight and surprise at this entrance of part of his dream into his very home. That entrance is later accentuated in the illustration depicting the blizzard that Mr. Popper has allowed to blow into his home. Drifts pile through the window, over an armchair, and across the floor, and children and penguins slide down them. When Mr. Popper takes Captain Cook out for a walk, he himself dresses like a penguin, as though somehow his dream has now merged with reality in such a way as to transform him.

But Lawson also captures the poignant side of Mr. Popper. When he first appears, he is burdened down with ladders, boards, cans of paint, and brushes; bits of wallpaper are stuck to him. He is in a very real sense trapped. Later, when he must decide the fate of the penguins, he appears old and defeated. The movie agent stands tall next to him, hands in pocket, chest thrust out, cigar clenched between teeth; he is confident and aggressive. Admiral Drake stands between the two men; although he, too, is self-assured, this is not because of his connections but simply because of who he is—the admiral. He is much taller than either of the men; they do not even come up to his shoulders. Mr. Popper is small, thin, crestfallen. He seems old and tired, and there is the sense here that he is comparing himself to these two men. He also realizes that should he send the penguins with Admiral Drake, there will be an end to even this manifestation of his dream.

The final joyous illustration, however, turns this around. Clothed in the garb of an arctic expedition, Mr. Popper waves from the side of the ship, both to his family and to the reader; one of the penguins waves with him. The expression is one of delight, the expression of someone who finds happiness unexpectedly. Here is humor mixed with poignancy, a suitable final illustration for this curious tale.

As Lawson moved into the early 1940s, he began to focus more on his own writing and illustrating and less on collaborative work. What he did do, however, showed how much he had learned about the art of illustration in the decade since he had begun illustrating children's books. In 1939 he illustrated a shortened form of John Bunyan's *Pilgrim's Progress*. To an uninspired text by Mary Godolphin, Lawson added uninspired characterization. But his backgrounds and landscape are rarely stronger in terms of their role in the narrative; not until *Rabbit Hill* would his background illustrations play as strong a role.

The cover illustration is busy and detailed, depicting Christian on one page and his family on the next, struggling through thorny woods. Trees grab at them, monstrous creatures watch, and the trail seems to disappear in the thickness of the brush, but still they push through. Their peaceful expressions belie the difficulties of the way, and they are drawn by a light in the upper left corner—a pictorial depiction of the overall theme of the book. The dark and dreary Slough of Despond, drawn like a cypress swamp, the wild yet ordered parklike setting of the Cross, the stately lines of the House Beautiful, the dark, shadowy things that crouch half-hidden in the Valley of the Shadow of Death, the pastoral scenery of the Land of Beulah, and the ethereal verticality of Zion—all are strong not in their depiction of characters, who are somewhat cartoonlike, but in their use of landscape and architecture to comment on and enlarge the story itself.

FROM *MR. POPPER'S PENGUINS* BY RICHARD AND FLORENCE ATWATER.
COPYRIGHT 1938 BY FLORENCE ATWATER AND RICHARD ATWATER; (C)
RENEWED 1966 BY FLORENCE ATWATER, DORIS ATWATER, AND CAR-
ROLL ATWATER BISHOP. BY PERMISSION OF LITTLE, BROWN AND CO.

The next year Lawson illustrated a collection of verse and stories entitled *Just for Fun* (1940), and one sees the enormous strides Lawson has taken since the earlier collections. Where before he had been literal and stilted, here the texts seem to free his imagination, so that the illustrations are light, full of whimsy, comic, and energetic. The opening illustration of a joyous Jonathan Bing dancing for spring sets the mood of the text; he is up on his toes with glee. Here are the kinds of pseudomedieval buildings that Lawson used in *Simpson and Sampson,* nonthreatening ogres who are upset over a change in fashion, benign dragons, and a feast that comes alive and rushes out the door. Everywhere there is movement and delight, whether it be in the fantasy illustrations or even in the more stately tales of Christmas Eve or of Saint Valentine, who is dressed as a Franciscan and walks with children dangling from each arm.

In 1943 Lawson illustrated Val Teal's strange short story *The Little Woman Wanted Noise,* published by the same publisher who had accepted *Just for Fun,* Rand McNally. Lawson uses the same format that he had used for Munro Leaf's books, but this slight story makes it difficult to extend or interpret the text. When a little woman who had lived in the city inherits a farm, she misses all of the noise that had given her such peace of mind. So she gathers together a collection of animals, then an old car, and finally goes back to the city to collect a couple of boys who, from then on, provide lots of noise. Lawson saves himself from simply repeating the accumulation of animals by picturing the growing collection at different sites on the farm, but he is hard-pressed to give them much to do. The most effective illustration is, once again, a landscape scene, recalling a similar scene in *They Were Strong and Good,* in which Lawson depicts the farmhouse and barn; the sense here is of utter calm and peace, and this, of course, lies at the point of the humorous irony that structures the book.

Perhaps the most successful long novel that Lawson illustrated—and certainly the only one outside his own texts remembered today—is Elizabeth Janet Gray's Newbery-winning *Adam of the Road* (1942). Lawson illustrates the title page of this thirteenth-century journey of a minstrel on the road with a drawing of Nick, the spaniel, and a minstrel's lyre. Where in Lawson's early work these title-page illustrations had been gratuitous, here he uses two of the central reasons Adam has for being on the road, as he searches for his missing dog and his missing father. Where Lawson had illustrated earlier historical novels with still tableaus, here his vision has led to illustrations filled with narrative movement. Characters are moving through wind, warming themselves by a fire in a great hall, confronting each other, sharing a lunch. Here is the first really successful fusion of detailed landscape and architecture with narrative action, as Lawson pictures not only the world of the novel—his earlier mode—but the action of the novel within that world.

In the 1930s Lawson had included full-color plates in several of his illustrated books: six in *The Wonderful Adventures of Little Prince Toofat,* six in *The Story of Jesus for Young People,* and one in *Swords and Statues,* for example. But in the late 1940s he ventured into full color, with Tom Robinson's *Greylock and the Robin* (1946) and *Dick Whittington and His Cat* (1949), which Lawson retold. *Greylock and the Robin* was a particularly unfortunate choice for Lawson; the story is simplistic and undramatic. While Greylock, a cat, watches from the bushes, a young robin falls from the clothesline into the lawn. As Greylock prepares to pounce, he is attacked by the robin's parents, who distract him until the young robin is able to escape to a nearby lilac. Although the setting is a familiar one to Lawson—a countryside scene, perhaps a farm—it plays a small role in the action. *Dick Whittington and His Cat* was much more successful. The focus of each of the illustrations is always on Dick. Lawson depicts his poverty by showing the frenzied activities of the huge rats that surround him as he sleeps. He shows his change of fortune as he sleeps with the cat who has killed the rats, illustrating a scene of peace and repose to counter the frenzied energy of the previous scene. At the end, Lawson shows Dick, still in rags, distributing his wealth to others, even to those who have persecuted him, and the expression is one of beatific peace.

In 1940 Lawson had written about the gathering of details for his illustrations: "The life of the average illustrator is an endless process of observing and storing away, in some curious rag-bag part of his mind, all the thousands of ill-assorted facts and impressions that he will sometime be called upon to use. He passes all his waking hours in what appears to be a sort of vacant daze, observing strange faces, how different sorts of shoes wrinkle, clothes, people, effects of light and shadow, how a plumber carries his tools, or what sort of horses draw milk wagons." In this letter Lawson shows his sense of the book as a whole package, as a single experience. From decoration to illustration, from tableau to narrative art, from stilted literalism to humorous extension of the text—this is Lawson's movement from apprenticeship to mastery. It is an apprenticeship filled with chances, experimentation, and innovation. It was that willingness to change and grow that led Lawson from commercial illustration to books like *Mr. Popper's Penguins* and *They Were Strong and Good.*

Chapter Seven

The Great Wheel: A Summing Up

The final year of Lawson's life saw two books: a revised edition of *Watchwords of Liberty* and *The Great Wheel*. They were, each in its own way, a culmination of his work in children's literature. *Watchwords of Liberty* is, like its 1943 predecessor, a celebration of American bravery and fortitude and accomplishments—another version, in a sense, of *They Were Strong and Good*. *The Great Wheel* is also a celebration of Americanness; here Lawson depicts the building of the first Ferris wheel, a gargantuan attraction that dwarfs the buildings and exhibits of the 1893 World's Columbian Exposition in Chicago. But even more, this book brings together all of the genres with which Lawson had experimented, concluding with the bucolic country scene that is always the seat of a marital bliss and fecundity in Lawson's work.

The Great Wheel was published posthumously; in fact, the first edition carries a line through the copyright notice by Robert Lawson and replaces it with another line of text above the canceled notice to indicate that the copyright is by Lawson's estate, suggesting that Lawson almost lived to see the final production of this, one of his finest works. Reviewers used language that was typical of a Lawson review, but most of them also noted the poignancy of the book. *The Great Wheel* is an America celebration, like *Watchwords of Liberty* and *They Were Strong and Good*. The celebration focuses on the American immigrants that Lawson would have seen in his youth, particularly the Irish and German immigrants who arrive with little and who, through hard work and undaunted spirit, make their way in this world. Their achievement is the Ferris wheel. The sheer size of the wheel, the colossal effrontery of it, the daringness of the engineer, the scale of the project—all are stuff of big America.

But *The Great Wheel* also represents a mixture of all of the genres with which Lawson had been experimenting for so long. It is the whimsical tale of a young boy who follows a fantastic dream—to seek the evening star and his destiny. In that sense, it is a journey like Mr. McWhinney's. But it is also a story of apprenticeship and growth, like *Smeller Martin*. And a fictionalized tale out of American history, like *Ben and Me* or *Mr.*

Revere and I. And a story about a search for home, like *Mr. Wilmer*—a home that would be in the country, as in *Rabbit Hill*. In short, *The Great Wheel* combines all of the themes that Lawson played, harmonizing them into a single piece.

The novel opens in Ireland, with an illustration in which Conn, the protagonist, sits on a stone wall, looking longingly out to sea. The illustration foretells the opening scene, for in it his Aunt Honora tells him that his fortune lies to the west. He should follow the evening star, she tells him, and one day he would ride the greatest wheel in the world. His mother despairs at this prophecy, but his grandfather points out poignantly that if Conn stayed in Ireland he would do nothing but cut peat all his life. His mother refuses to be consoled. And she has reason to lament, for six years later, when Conn is eighteen, a letter comes from his uncle in New York, offering him a position in his construction company. Conn's response to the news is divided, but he will go: "His fortune was calling loudly now, the shimmering golden road to the west spread before him. His heart leaped with the thrill of great changes to come."[1] The next day he is on a ship, sailing to New York City.

Aboard ship he meets Trudy, a German immigrant traveling with her family to Wisconsin; he falls in love, and she predicts that they will meet again if he continues to follow his aunt's fortune. Neither has a sense of the geography of the country. But while Trudy heads west, Conn settles into life in New York, where he is quickly accepted into his Uncle Michael's family and is adored by his two cousins. He is quick at learning and soon becomes an indispensable part of his uncle's business, which is mostly centered on building sewers. On his days off, he wanders New York, befriending an old ship rigger. And he seems quite happy. But he is not following the evening star.

When his Uncle Patrick comes calling, Conn sees his chance. This uncle also works in construction but on a much larger scale. He promises travel, adventure, and work on one of the marvels of the age: a great, huge wheel to be exhibited at the Columbian Exposition in Chicago, built by Mr. Ferris. Conn, against the advice of Uncle Michael, gives up the security of his New York position and travels to Chicago, where he will work—outside an office—and be closer to Trudy in Wisconsin. He does not know her last name, nor her address, but he begins to write letters to her, describing his feelings about the wonderful project of which he is now a part.

With Uncle Michael's brawling assistant, Conn's quick skills, and Mr. Ferris' genius, the huge wheel begins to go up. Conn's friend Mar-

tin, the ship's rigger, has also come, and he, too, shows a kind of genius in assembling the wheel. Despite the insistence of other engineers that a wheel on this scale cannot be constructed, the project goes forward, funded by businessmen like Mr. Zillheimer, whose faith in Mr. Ferris is undaunted by the warnings of others. Conn becomes deeply immersed in the project, realizing that it is the fulfillment of his aunt's prophecy. He also hopes and believes that someday Trudy will come to the fair to ride it.

The footings are dug and poured, the sides constructed, the axle put into place, and then work on the wheel itself begins. The crews working on the wheel compete, and when the last bolt is tightened, they all realize they have achieved something amazing. The cars arrive—each one big enough to hold 60 people—and are attached, and Mr. Ferris prepares to head south to a bridge-building project. He invites Conn, who has also proved his worth on the job, to come with him. But Conn is reluctant. He knows that bridge-building is not his destiny. He wants something else: "A farm, maybe. . . . But anyway some place of my own, the way you can be driving a nail to hang your overalls on and know

that tomorrow and the next month and the next year the same nail'll be
there in the same place" (129).

And truth to tell, Conn still waits for Trudy. Mr. Ferris understands
and also recognizes that Conn cannot let the wheel out of his life quite
yet. Conn becomes a uniformed attendant in Car Number One, an elegant plush car that Mr. and Mrs. Ferris ride for the first time. Conn,
delighted with his position, attends the car all summer and into the fall,
conveying thousands of riders in and out, always watching for Trudy.
During the late summer Uncle Michael and his cousins visit, but Conn
will not return with them, despite a clear proposal of marriage from one
of his cousins and the offer of an eventual partnership. Finally, in the fall,
not long before the wheel is to be torn down as the fair concludes, Trudy
comes.

But she is not what he expected at all. She comes with Mr. Zillheimer, and Conn discovers that she is one of his nieces and quite
wealthy. She insists that she is no different from the way she had been on
the immigrant boat, that she must work as hard as anyone, but Conn
does not believe her. He is crushed; she, however, begins a campaign of
sorts, coming each day to ride the wheel, knitting an elaborate sweater
with a picture of a farm. Martin finally intervenes, giving Trudy the
stacks of letters that Conn had been writing all summer long. When
Trudy finally finishes the sweater and holds it up to him, her vision is
clear, and they are reconciled.

Soon they are married. They travel to Wisconsin to learn the cheese
business and settle down on a farm; Conn's westward journey has been
completed. The scene is idyllic, and then perfectly complete when several of Mr. Zillheimer's horses come into view, carting Car Number One
from the dismantled great wheel. He had dreamed of one day living in it
as a house for he and Trudy, and when she reminds him of this, he suggests that now it might be used for a playhouse: "I'm suited where I
am" (188).

Conn's movement from the peat bogs of Ireland to his farm in Wisconsin is Robert Lawson's depiction of the American Dream. Here is his
celebration of everything he had celebrated in *They Were Strong and Good,*
and the novel functions in much the same way: Lawson again combines
a focus on the individual and the communal experience. On the one
hand Lawson focuses on the fictional character, Conn, the Irish immigrant, who through his wit, native skill, and desire to follow his dream
in the end finds love and contentment. His dream is not to become the
millionaire but to find a place of his own where he can work hard and be

strong and good and have many children. On the other hand Lawson is depicting the immigrant experience—one he did not live firsthand but would have observed. This is the story of the Irish immigrant who comes with no resources and who is yet able to thrive as part of American society; it is the story of the immigrant who comes desiring what he cannot find in Ireland—land he can call his own and the opportunity to decide how he or she shall live. In the midst of a cold war, these are the American values Lawson chooses to highlight in *The Great Wheel*.

As the title suggests, the wheel is the novel's central symbol. It is the goal toward which Conn moves in the beginning of the book, the consuming dream that he helps to build in the center of the story, and the symbol of his success at the conclusion. His success comes as he decides to have faith in the prophecy that his aunt has given, but it also comes about because of his faith in the massive technology of a sprawling young nation that dares to build what has never before been built. One evening, while Conn is at work on the wheel, he hears an old spiritual rise up from the Pullman porters, and its words are peculiarly appropriate for him:

> And the little wheel ran by faith
> And the big wheel ran by the grace of God.
> It's a wheel in a wheel
> Way up in the middle of the air. (141)

Conn's reaction is a complex one. On the one hand his faith lies in technology; he believes in the Great Wheel; it is a sign of the possibilities of the country. And he believes in Mr. Ferris, as do the other workmen. Certainly in this sense the wheel symbolizes the potential of American engineering might. But the song also calls up something else in Conn: "What was it that had shown so steadily in Trudy's eyes that last evening on the ship as she said with such serene certainty, 'I will wait and you will come, it is your fortune'?" (143). There is a large sense here of overriding destiny, that he is a wheel within a larger wheel, and that his fortune is within the auspices of that larger wheel. On the communal level, this faith suggests a nation's sense of itself as fulfilling a destiny that is itself ordained. Within a very short time, it would be hard to imagine writing a book with such a stance.

On a structural level, Lawson has moved back to a technique he had used in *Rabbit Hill:* find a central symbol that is crucial to the novel's plot line and meaning and build the narrative around that. With *Rabbit Hill* it had been the house and gardens; with *The Great Wheel* it is the wheel itself. It is the focus of American ingenuity, of Conn's prophetic journey, and even of love. Like its spokes, it draws and organizes each of the disparate elements of the novel.

That central symbol so dominates the book, so straddles its narrative that the characters are all one-dimensional. And in this, *The Great Wheel* is typical of Lawson's work: his settings are developed, multifaceted, layered with meaning, but his characters lack this complexity. The two uncles whom Conn meets in America are both marked by an aggressive industry that is more or less boisterous. Mr. Zillheimer is the successful immigrant pleased at the yield of his hard work. Trudy is the loving woman who identifies her life with home and children. And even Conn, the protagonist, is relatively simply drawn. He follows his dream westward, a drive made possible by his perseverance and sense of destiny. His combination of a drive for adventure with a drive for his own home makes him unique among the characters of this novel, but not complex. In fact, his very simplicity seems to be an important part of his character.

Conn's characterization is suggested by the frontispiece. All of the principal characters are pictured here, with Conn the most prominent. He stares across the page at Trudy, who represents the one thing for which he truly yearns. In fact, each of the characters seems to yearn for only one thing, whether it is rigging or an engineering marvel or Conn himself—and the great wheel plays a large role in deciding whether those decisions are realized. As if to suggest this role, Lawson puts the Great Wheel over the portraits of the frontispiece, so that is seems to dominate them. But like Conn, the star that Conn follows stands apart, as if to suggest that what he follows is even greater than the Great Wheel. The wheel, for Conn, is in the end only a way toward something larger.

The first illustration in the text itself is that of Conn gazing out toward the ocean; clearly his own dream began before his aunt's prophecy, and this is important to the larger theme of Lawson's work. His vision of the American dream is not one of simple destiny or prophecy; instead, destiny becomes reality only insofar as it is worked for and in fact produced. The illustration that depicts Father Riley reading the letter that sends Conn to America makes this same suggestion, for although Conn's extended family is all there listening, all underneath a mantle picture of the Statue of Liberty, Conn is not present. In a sense, he has already left this family to which he will never return, a leaving that his mother already recognizes.

The Great Wheel came close to bringing Lawson his second Newbery; it came in behind Harold Keith's *Rifles for Watie,* another story of America. It is Lawson's tightest and least episodic novel. The speech of the characters with its Irish lilt, the illustrations of confident and hardworking figures, the scale of the wheel, the movement from east to west—all this comes together to portray one moment in American history, in much the same way that the Columbian Exposition did in 1893. And above this story is Conn's tale—one that typifies the American Dream as it was imagined in 1957. In this sense, *The Great Wheel* represents the summing up of Lawson's literary career.

Lawson had started his career in the glow of Arthur Rackham's work. He had begun with faerie, with the fanciful figures of Rackham's prints. By the time of *The Great Wheel,* however, he had long left that tradition behind. Even in his whimsical works and historical fantasies, Lawson had turned to scrupulously realistic illustrations in terms of backgrounds. If his characters are flying in a bicycle, they are nevertheless flying over a dam drawn with complete accuracy. If they are riding a talking horse, they are riding against a rigorously detailed New England landscape. The fancy of Rackham has no place in the work of Lawson's later, more mature illustration.

Lawson's work is most akin to two contemporaries: Robert McCloskey and James Daugherty. McCloskey, too, used line drawings and experimented with genre; Daugherty, like Lawson, wrote about the American experience, although his focus was principally on the nineteenth-century westward movement. As the 1960s approached, so Lawson's writing about America languished and went out of print. But the Rabbit Hill books, as well as *The Story of Ferdinand,* continue with only slightly abated popularity.

If one was to look for Lawson's continuing influence, it would lie with his pioneering work in the fusion of realism with fantasy. Instead of using J. R. R. Tolkien's definition of fantasy as the creation of an "other," secondary world—a definition that Arthur Rackham would have affirmed—Lawson created fantasy in the very real primary world— apparently ordinary but ripe with astonishing possibilities. That same fusion is seen today principally in the work of illustrators: Audrey and Don Wood's *Elbert's Bad Word* (1988); Chris Van Allsburg's *Jumanji* (1981), *Just a Dream* (1990), and *The Polar Express* (1985); David Wiesner's *Hurricane* (1990), *Free Fall* (1988), and *Tuesday* (1991); Dennis Nolan's *The Castle Builder* (1987); and Allen Say's *A River Dream* (1988) and *Stranger in the Mirror* (1995).

It is not influence, however, for which Lawson will be remembered. It is his gentle rabbits, his pacific bull, his irascible mouse, his comic penguins. These are his legacy, his works that may someday be called classics or, depending on critical schools, touchstones. It would probably not have displeased him that he is today known more for his illustration than for his writing; in his own eyes he was always more the illustrator than the writer, always more the drawer of narrative pictures than the crafter of text.

Notes and References

Preface

1. Helen L. Jones, *Robert Lawson, Illustrator: A Selection of His Character-istic Illustrations* (Boston: Little, Brown, 1972), 92; hereafter cited in text.

2. *They Were Strong and Good* (New York: Viking, 1940), n.p.; hereafter cited in text.

3. "Make Me a Child Again," *Horn Book* 16 (November–December, 1940): 44456; hereafter cited in text as "Make Me."

Chapter One

1. "The Newbery Award Acceptance," *Horn Book* 21 (July–August 1945): 234; hereafter cited in text as "Newbery."

2. "Robert Lawson," *Horn Book* 17 (July–August 1941): 285; hereafter cited in text as "Robert Lawson."

3. *Magazine of the Junior Heritage Club*, n.d; quoted in Annette H. Weston, "Robert Lawson: Author and Illustrator," *Elementary English* 47 (January 1970): 74–84; hereafter cited in text.

4. Marie A. Lawson, "Master of Rabbit Hill: Robert Lawson," *Horn Book* 21 (July–August 1945): 240; hereafter cited in text.

5. Cited in Jones, 52. See also Rose Henderson, "Robert Lawson—Master of Fantasy," Sunday Magazine Section, *New York Herald Tribune*, 30 November 1930, 14–15; hereafter cited in text.

6. This etching is reproduced in Jones, 1.

7. "The Caldecott Medal Acceptance," *Horn Book* 17 (July–August 1941): 274; hereafter cited in text as "Caldecott."

8. From a speech delivered to the Scottish Branch of the English Association, 22 November 1930. Cited in Ann Commire, ed., "Robert Lawson," *Yesterday's Authors of Books for Children,* vol. 2 (Detroit: Gale Research, 1978), 232–34.

9. Margaret Leaf, "Happy Birthday, Ferdinand!" *Publishers Weekly,* 31 October 1986, 33; hereafter cited in text.

10. "Lo, the Poor Illustrator," *Publishers Weekly,* December 1935, 2092–94.

11. Frederick R. Gardner, *Robert Lawson on My Shelves* (Philadelphia: Free Library of Philadelphia, 1977), 8.

12. Michael Patrick Hearn, "Ferdinand the Bull's 50th Anniversary," *Washington Post Book World,* 9 November 1986, 13, 22; hereafter cited in text.

13. "Bull Market Soars as Ferdinand Becomes Commercial Product," *Life,* 28 November 1938, 34. This page was followed by three full-color pages from the Disney short film.

14. Ernest Hemingway, "The Faithful Bull," *Holiday,* March 1951, 51.

15. Letter from Robert Lawson to Little, Brown, July 1941, and letter from Robert Lawson to Little, Brown, December 1951; in Jones, 81.

16. Letter from Robert Lawson to Little, Brown, 3 April 1954; in Jones, 86.

17. Letter from Robert Lawson to Helen Jones, September 1942; in Jones, 65.

18. Speech for the BBC Children's Hour, 4 May 1946; cited in Weston, 81.

19. Letter from Robert Lawson to Helen Jones, 27 July 1943; in Jones, 35.

20. Jennie Lindquist, "The Master of Rabbit Hill," *Horn Book* 33 (August 1957): 273.

Chapter Two

1. J. E. Stromdahl, review of *They Were Strong and Good, Library Journal* 65 (1 November 1940): 926.

2. Review of *They Were Strong and Good, Catholic World* 152 (December 1940): 373.

3. A. M. Jordan, review of *They Were Strong and Good, Horn Book* 16 (November 1940): 437.

4. F.B. Sloan, review of *They Were Strong and Good, Christian Science Monitor,* 11 November 1940, 9.

5. A. T. Eaton, review of *They Were Strong and Good, New York Times Book Review,* 10 November 1940, 10.

6. *Watchwords of Liberty: A Pageant of American Quotations* (Boston: Little, Brown, 1943); hereafter cited in text.

7. *Watchwords of Liberty: A Pageant of American Quotations,* rev. ed. (Boston: Little, Brown, 1957), 112.

Chapter Three

1. *I Discover Columbus* (Boston: Little, Brown, 1941), viii; hereafter cited in text.

2. *Ben and Me* (Boston: Little, Brown, 1939), 68; hereafter cited in text.

3. Review of *I Discover Columbus, Books,* 2 November 1941, 7; Alice Jordan, review of *I Discover Columbus, Horn Book* 17 (September 1941): 366; review of *I Discover Columbus, New York Times Book Review,* 2 October 1941, 7; review of *I Discover Columbus, New Yorker,* 6 December 1941, 144.

4. Review of *I Discover Columbus, New York Times Book Review,* 7.

5. *Mr. Revere and I* (Boston: Little, Brown, 1953), 5; hereafter cited in text.

6.   *Captain Kidd's Cat* (Boston: Little, Brown, 1956), 4; hereafter cited in text.

Chapter Four

1.   Review of *Rabbit Hill, Saturday Review of Literature* 27 (9 December 1944): 32–33.

2.   *Rabbit Hill* (New York: Viking Press, 1944); hereafter cited in text.

3.   Anne Eaton, review of *Rabbit Hill, New York Times Book Review,* 15 October 1944, 12; review of *Rabbit Hill, Saturday Review of Literature,* 32–33.

4.   Review of *Rabbit Hill, Horn Book* 20 (November 1944): 487.

5.   Review of *Rabbit Hill, New Yorker,* 16 December 1944, 84.

6.   Review of *Robbut: A Tale of Tails, Kirkus Review* 16 (15 August 1948): 397; review of *Robbut: A Tale of Tails, New York Times Book Review,* 14 November 1948, 60; review of *Robbut: A Tale of Tails, Saturday Review of Literature* 31 (13 November 1948): 24.

7.   *Robbut: A Tale of Tails* (New York: Viking Press, 1948), 26–28; hereafter cited in text.

8.   *Edward, Hoppy and Joe* (New York: Alfred A. Knopf, 1952); hereafter cited in text.

9.   Quoted in Anne Carroll Moore, "The Three Owls' Notebook," *Horn Book* 30 (December 1954): 413.

10.   Jennie Lindquist, review of *The Tough Winter, Horn Book* 30 (October 1954): 343; Nancy Jane Day, review of *The Tough Winter, Saturday Review of Literature* 37 (13 November 1954): 74; C. Elta Van Norman, review of *The Tough Winter, New York Times Book Review,* 14 November 1954, 2.

11.   *The Tough Winter* (New York: Viking Press, 1954), 128; hereafter cited in text.

Chapter Five

1.   *Mr. Wilmer* (Boston: Little, Brown, 1945), 2; hereafter cited in text.

2.   *Mr. Twigg's Mistake* (Boston: Little, Brown, 1947), 30; hereafter cited in text.

3.   *The Fabulous Flight* (Boston: Little, Brown, 1949), 75; hereafter cited in text.

4.   In a letter to Helen Jones, Lawson wrote that "that particular gargoyle has been done by every etcher for the past hundred years or so and I think my version stands up very well as compared to most of them" (26 May 1948; in Jones, 45).

5.   *Smeller Martin* (New York: Viking Press, 1950), 14; hereafter cited in text.

6.   *McWhinney's Jaunt* (Boston: Little, Brown, 1951), 3; hereafter cited in text.

Chapter Six

1. Margery Williams Bianco, *The Hurdy-Gurdy Man* (New York: Oxford University Press, 1933), 33.

2. Barbara Ring, *Peik,* trans. Lorence Munson Woodside (Boston: Little, Brown, 1932), 37.

3. See, for example, Jean Streufert Patrick, "Robert Lawson's *The Story of Ferdinand*: Death in the Afternoon or Life under the Cork Tree?," in *Touchstones: Reflections on the Best in Children's Literature,* vol. 3. ed. Perry Nodelman (West Lafayette, Ind.: Children's Literature Association, 1989), 74–84, which investigates Lawson's use of irony in *The Story of Ferdinand* and argues for a gendered interpretation of the book.

4. Munro Leaf, *The Story of Ferdinand* (New York: Viking Press, 1936), n.p.

5. Munro Leaf, *The Story of Simpson and Sampson* (New York: Viking Press, 1941), n.p.

6. Munro Leaf, *Wee Gillis* (New York: Viking Press, 1938), n.p.

7. Andrew Lang, *Prince Prigio* (Boston: Little, Brown, 1942).

Chapter Seven

1. *The Great Wheel* (New York: Viking Press, 1957), 16; hereafter cited in text.

Selected Bibliography

PRIMARY WORKS

Works Written and Illustrated

At That Time. *New York: Viking, 1947.*
Ben and Me. *Boston: Little, Brown, 1939.*
Captain Kidd's Cat. *Boston: Little, Brown, 1956.*
Country Colic. *Boston: Little, Brown, 1944.*
Dick Whittington and His Cat. *New York: Limited Editions Club, 1949.*
Edward, Hoppy and Joe. *New York: Knopf, 1952.*
The Fabulous Flight. *Boston: Little, Brown, 1949.*
The Great Wheel. *New York: Viking, 1957.*
I Discover Columbus. *Boston: Little, Brown, 1941.*
Just for Fun: A Collection of Stories and Verses. *Chicago: Rand McNally, 1940.*
McWhinney's Jaunt. *Boston: Little, Brown, 1951.*
Mr. Revere and I. *Boston: Little, Brown, 1953.*
Mr. Twigg's Mistake. *Boston: Little, Brown, 1947.*
Mr. Wilmer. *Boston: Little, Brown, 1945.*
Rabbit Hill. *New York: Viking, 1944.*
Robbut: A Tale of Tails. *New York: Viking, 1948.*
Smeller Martin. *New York: Viking, 1950.*
They Were Strong and Good. *New York: Viking, 1940; rev. ed., 1968.*
The Tough Winter. *New York: Viking, 1954.*
Watchwords of Liberty. *Boston: Little, Brown, 1943; rev. ed., 1957.*

Works Illustrated

Atwater, Richard, and Florence Atwater. *Mr. Popper's Penguins.* Boston: Little, Brown, 1938.
Barnes, Ruth A., ed. *I Hear America Singing: An Anthology of Folk Poetry.* Chicago: John C. Winston Co. and the Junior Literary Guild, 1937.
Bates, Helen Dixon. *Betsy Ross.* New York: Whittlesey House and McGraw-Hill, 1936.
_____. *Francis Scott Key.* New York: Whittlesey House and McGraw-Hill, 1936.
Bianco, Margery Williams. "The House That Grew Small." *Saint Nicholas Magazine* 58 (September 1931): 764–66, 782–83.
_____. *The Hurdy-Gurdy Man.* New York: Oxford University Press, 1933.

Bowie, Walter Russell. *The Story of Jesus for Young People.* New York: Charles Scribner's Sons, 1937.

Brewton, John E. *Gaily We Parade: A Collection of Poems about People, Here, There and Everywhere.* New York: Macmillan, 1940.

———. *Under the Tent of the Sky: A Collection of Poems about Animals Large and Small.* New York: Macmillan, 1937.

Bunyan, John. *Pilgrim's Progress.* Text revised by Mary Godolphin. Philadelphia: J. B. Lippincott, 1939.

Chester, George Randolph. *The Wonderful Adventures of Little Prince Toofat.* New York: James A. McCann, 1922.

Coatsworth, Elizabeth. *The Golden Horseshoe.* New York: Macmillan, 1935; rev. ed., 1968.

Cormack, Maribelle. *Wind of the Vikings: A Tale of the Orkney Isles.* New York: D. Appleton-Century, 1937.

Dickens, Charles. *A Tale of Two Cities.* Boston: Ginn, 1938.

Farjeon, Eleanor. *One Foot in Fairyland.* New York: F. A. Stokes, 1938.

Fish, Helen Dean, ed. *Four and Twenty Blackbirds: Nursery Rhymes of Yesterday Recalled for Children of To-Day.* Philadelphia: J. B. Lippincott, 1937.

Forester, C. S. *Poo-Poo and the Dragons.* Boston: Little, Brown, 1942.

Gale, Elizabeth. *Seven Beads of Wampum.* New York: G. P. Putnam's Sons, 1936.

Glenn, Mabelle, et al., eds. *Tunes and Harmonies.* New York: G. P. Putnam's Sons, 1936.

Gray, Elizabeth Janet. *Adam of the Road.* New York: Viking, 1942.

Haines, William Wister. *High Tension.* Boston: Little, Brown, 1938.

———. *Slim.* Boston: Little, Brown, 1934.

Hall, William. *The Shoelace Robin.* New York: Thomas Y. Crowell, 1945.

Kissin, Rita. *Pete the Pelican.* Philadelphia: J. B. Lippincott, 1937.

Lang, Andrew. *Prince Prigio.* Boston: Little, Brown, 1942.

Leaf, Munro. *Aesop's Fables.* New York: Heritage Press, 1941.

———. *The Story of Ferdinand.* New York: Viking Press, 1936.

———. *The Story of Simpson and Sampson.* New York: Viking Press, 1941.

———. *Wee Gillis.* New York: Viking Press, 1938.

Marquand, John P. *Haven's End.* Boston: Little, Brown, 1933.

Mason, Arthur. *From the Horn of the Moon.* Garden City, N.Y.: Doubleday, Doran, 1931. Excerpted as "Moving of the Bog," *Saint Nicholas Magazine* 58 (July 1931): 644–47, 667–70.

———. *The Roving Lobster.* Garden City, N.Y.: Doubleday, Doran, 1931.

———. *The Wee Men of Ballywooden.* Garden City, N.Y.: Doubleday, Doran, 1930; New York: Viking Press, 1952.

Neilson, Frances F., and Winthrop Neilson. *Benjamin Franklin.* Reader in Real People Series. New York: Row, Peterson, 1950.

Potter, Mary A., et al. *Mathematics for Success.* Boston: Ginn, 1952.

Ring, Barbara. *Peik.* Translated by Lorence Munson Woodside. Boston: Little, Brown, 1932.

Robinson, Tom. *Greylock and the Robins*. New York: Viking Press and the Junior
    Literary Guild, 1946.
Rosmer, Jean. *In Secret Service: A Mystery Story of Napoleon's Court*. Translated by
    Virginia Olcott. Philadelphia: J. B. Lippincott, 1937.
Stephens, James. *The Crock of Gold*. New York: Limited Editions Club, 1942.
Sterne, Emma Gelders. *Drums of Monmouth*. New York: Dodd, Mead & Co.,
    1936.
_____. *Miranda Is a Princess: A Story of Old Spain*. New York: Dodd, Mead &
    Co., 1937.
Stratton, Clarence. *Swords and Statues: A Tale of Sixteenth Century Italy*. New
    York: John C. Winston Co. and the Junior Literary Guild, 1937.
Tarn, William Woodthorpe. *The Treasure of the Isle of Mist*. New York: G. P. Put-
    nam's Sons, 1934.
Teal, Val. *The Little Woman Wanted Noise*. New York: Rand McNally, 1943; rev.
    ed., 1967.
Twain, Mark. *The Prince and the Pauper*. Chicago: John C. Winston Co., 1937.
Untermeyer, Louis. "The Donkey of God." *Saint Nicholas Magazine* 59 (Decem-
    ber 1931): 59–61, 105–108.
White, T. H. *The Sword in the Stone*. New York: G. P. Putnam's Sons, 1939.
Young, Ella. *The Unicorn with Silver Shoes*. New York: Longmans, Green, 1932.

Articles and Writings about Children's Literature

"The Art of Caldecott and Greenaway." *New York Times Book Review*, 17 March
    1946, 7.
"The Caldecott Medal Acceptance." *Horn Book* 17 (July–August 1941):
    273–84. Reprinted as "On Children and Books," *Childhood Education* 18
    (February 1942): 268–73.
"The Genius of Arthur Rackham." *Horn Book* 16 (May–June 1940): 147–51.
"Howard Pyle and His Times." In *Illustrators of Children's Books, 1744–1945*,
    edited by Bertha E. Mahony, Louise Payson Latimer, and Beulah Folms-
    bee, 103–22. Boston: Horn Book, 1947.
"It Was a Nice, Simple Idea." *Publishers Weekly*, 10 July 1943.
"Lo, the Poor Illustrator." *Publishers Weekly*, December 1935, 2092–94.
"Make Me a Child Again." *Horn Book* 16 (November–December 1940):
    447–56. Reprinted in *Something Shared: Children and Books*, edited by
    Phyllis Fenner, 44–53. New York: John Day Co., 1959.
"The Newbery Medal Acceptance." *Horn Book* 21 (July–August 1945):
    233–38.
"The Powder Town." *Harper's Weekly*, 4 December 1915, 542.
"Robert Lawson." *Horn Book* 17 (July–August 1941): 285–88.
"Robert Lawson Answers the 'Menace' of the Comics." *Chicago Sunday Tribune*,
    11 November 1949.

Collection

The largest, most significant collection of Robert Lawson's materials lies in the Frederick R. Gardner Collection of the Free Library of Philadelphia.

SECONDARY WORKS

Biographical Studies

"Bull Market Soars as Ferdinand Becomes Commercial Product." *Life,* 28 November 1938, 34.

Cart, Michael. "Ben, Mr. Popper and the Rabbits: Remembering Robert Lawson." *New York Times Book Review,* 13 November 1988, 59.

Checklist of Drawings and Watercolors (1922–1957) for Books Illustrated by Robert Lawson. Frederick R. Gardner Collection. Philadelphia: Free Library of Philadelphia, 1977.

Gardner, Frederick R. *Robert Lawson on My Shelves.* Philadelphia: Free Library of Philadelphia, 1977.

Hearn, Michael Patrick. "Ferdinand the Bull's 50th Anniversary." *Washngton Post Book World,* 9 November 1986, 13, 22.

Henderson, Rose. "Robert Lawson—Master of Fantasy." Sunday Magazine Section. *New York Herald Tribune,* 30 November 1930, 14–15.

Lawson, Marie. "Master of Rabbit Hill: Robert Lawson." *Horn Book* 21 (July–August 1945): 233–38.

Leaf, Margaret. "Happy Birthday, Ferdinand!" *Publishers Weekly,* 31 October 1986, 33.

Lindquist, Jennie L. "The Master of Rabbit Hill." *Horn Book* 33 (August 1957): 273.

Massee, May. "Robert Lawson, 1940 Caldecott Winner." *Library Journal* 66 (July 1941): 591–92.

Smith, Irene. "Newbery and Caldecott Award Winners." *American Library Association Bulletin* (July 1941): 422–49.

Critical Studies

Burns, Mary Mehlman. " 'There Is Enough for All': Robert Lawson's America." 3 parts. *Horn Book* 48 (February 1972): 24–32; 48 (April 1972): 120–28; 48 (June 1972): 295–305. In examining the American values that Lawson's books espouse and celebrate, Burns argues that his work is about the ways in which "homely virtues" are part of the American experience. She follows this argument through the early fantasies that Lawson illustrated, the historical fantasies, and the Rabbit Hill books, concluding that the most important value that Lawson expresses is the fecundity of the country, the sense that there is enough for all.

Fish, Helen Dean. "Robert Lawson—Illustrator in the Great Tradition." *Horn Book* 16 (January–February 1940): 16–26. Reprinted in *Caldecott Medal Books, 1938–1957,* edited by Bertha Mahoney Miller and Elinoir Whitney Field. Boston: Horn Book, 1957. Fish argues that in many senses, Lawson was a nineteenth-century illustrator, in that the sources for and influences on his work are from the Victorian illustrators such as Arthur Rackham; this is particulalry true of his early work, but continued, she argues, through his career.

Jones, Helen L., ed. *Robert Lawson, Illustrator: A Selection of His Characteristic Illustrations.* Boston: Little, Brown, 1972. Included in this collection of 100 Lawson illustrations—some from his well-known volumes, some from obscure collaborations, and some etchings—are quotes from letters sent between Lawson's editors at Little, Brown and himself. In particular, Jones focuses on the process of Lawson's work.

Madson, Valden J. "Classic Americana: Themes and Values in the Tales of Robert Lawson." *Lion and the Unicorn* 3 (Spring 1979): 89–106. In this personal essay, Madson reflects on his first readings of books such as *Mr. Revere and I* and *Rabbit Hill.*

Patrick, Jean Streufert. "Robert Lawson's *The Story of Ferdinand:* Death in the Afternoon or Life under the Cork Tree?" In *Touchstones: Reflections on the Best in Children's Literature,* vol. 3, edited by Perry Nodelman, 74–84. West Lafayette, Ind.: Children's Literature Association, 1989. Patrick examines the role of Lawson's illustrations in *The Story of Ferdinand,* exploring particularly their use of irony, their connection to Hemingway's *Death in the Afternoon,* and their play with traditional male standards.

Sicherman, R. "Appreciation of Robert Lawson." *Elementary English* 44 (December 1967): 866–69, 874. In this short personal appreciation, Sicherman focuses on Lawson's keen awareness of his audience of child readers, and his sense that his work was aimed at them both textually and pictorially.

Steig, Michael. "Ferdinand and Wee Gillis at Half-Century." *Children's Literature Association Quarterly* 14 (Fall 1989): 118–23. Steig insightfully argues that Wee Gillis and Ferdinand the bull, both as they appear in their texts and in Lawson's illustrations, are connected through their rejections of the typical roles that they are expected to fulfill. The conclusion of each of these works is marked by the assertion of independence.

Weston, Annette H. "Robert Lawson: Author and Illustrator." *Elementary English* 47 (January 1970): 74–84. Reprinted in *Authors and Illustrators of Children's Books,* edited by Miriam Hoffman and Eva Samuels, 256–67. New Providence, N.J.: Bowker, 1972. One of the finest sources of Lawson quotations from his oral speeches and interviews, this article is divided between a biographical and a critical section, the first focusing particularly on his career as illustrator, the second probing the union of his texts and illustrations.

Index

The Author

Gary D. Schmidt received his B.A. from Gordon College, Wenham, Massachusetts, and his M.A. and Ph.D. in medieval literature from the University of Illinois at Urbana-Champaign. A professor of English at Calvin College, Grand Rapids, Michigan, he teaches children's literature, medieval literature, and the history of the English language. He has co-edited two collections of essays by children's literature critics and authors: *The Voice of the Narrator in Children's Literature* (1989; with Charlotte F. Otten) and *Sitting at the Feet of the Past: The Retelling of the North American Folktale* (1992; with Donald R. Hettinga). The author of *Robert McCloskey* (1990), *Hugh Lofting* (1992), and *Katherine Paterson* (1994), Schmidt has ventured into the writing of children's literature with a retelling of *Pilgrim's Progress,* illustrated by Barry Moser (1994); *The Sin Eater* (1996); and *The Blessing of the Lord,* illustrated by Dennis Nolan (1997).

The Editor

Ruth K. MacDonald is college dean for the I Have a Dream Foundation in Hartford, Connecticut. She received her B.A. and M.A. in English from the University of Connecticut, her Ph.D. in English from Rutgers University, and her M.B.A. from the University of Texas at El Paso. She is the author of the volumes on Louisa May Alcott, Beatrix Potter, and Dr. Seuss in Twayne's United States Authors and English Authors series and of the books *Literature for Children in England and America, 1646–1774* (1982) and *Christian's Children: The Influence of John Bunyan's "Pilgrim's Progress" on American Children's Literature* (1989).